T0020554

"Our questions really matter. Yet o[...] seek for the truth and not just end [...] conversation at our query. That's what J.D. Greear does here. He asks the questions—and proposes clear answers—about key issues of the Christian faith. *Essential Christianity* will be a key resource for those considering the faith and for their friends who want to share it with them."

ED STETZER, Executive Director, The Billy Graham Center, Wheaton College, Illinois

"My heart was skipping with excitement as I read this book. J.D. writes with simplicity and grip—he teaches clearly because he understands deeply. This book will show you a devastating critique of the human condition that will ring true to your experience of life; and then it will reveal to you the overwhelming wonder of God's solution in Jesus Christ. Whether you are an honest seeker or a mature pilgrim, I cannot commend this book highly enough to you."

RICO TICE, Founder, Christianity Explored Ministries; Senior Minister, All Souls Langham Place, London

"If you're wondering what on earth to believe in a confusing and often disappointing world, *Essential Christianity* could be just the lifeline you need. In it, pastor J.D. Greear peels back the layers that can get piled on top of Christianity and helps us see the 1st-century original, which offers life-changing hope to billions around the world today—including you."

REBECCA MCLAUGHLIN, Author, *Confronting Christianity: 12 Hard Questions for the World's Largest Religion*

"J.D. Greear has a rare gift for really getting into the mind of the modern skeptic. He gets out in front of every key question and objection to Christianity and answers each one with compassion, honesty, and a great sense of humor. I bet even the surliest and most self-assured atheist wouldn't mind sitting next to Greear on a plane—and would never be quite the same after their conversation."

MOLLY WORTHEN, Associate Professor of History, University of North Carolina; *New York Times* columnist; Author, *Apostles of Reason: The Crisis of Authority in American Evangelicalism*

"Every generation needs a voice to present the central tenets of the Christian faith in a way that is both contemporary and timeless. With *Essential Christianity*, J.D. Greear shares the good news using simple, direct language and explanations first laid out by the apostle Paul. A compelling and helpful guide for anyone exploring their own faith journey."

DAN CATHY, Chairman, Chick-fil-A

ESSENTIAL CHRISTIANITY

J.D. GREEAR

To my mother, Carol, who went home to be with the Lord during the writing of this book. Because of you, Mom, from childhood I have "been acquainted with the sacred writings, which are able to make [someone] wise for salvation through faith in Christ Jesus" (2 Timothy 3:15).

And to Steve Roberson, who faithfully called me back to Christ during my high school years.

And to Tim Keller, who taught me to love the gospel all over again, and that (as Martin Luther said), "to progress in the Christian life is always to begin again."

Essential Christianity
© J.D. Greear, 2023
Published by:
The Good Book Company

thegoodbook.com | thegoodbook.co.uk
thegoodbook.com.au | thegoodbook.co.nz | thegoodbook.co.in

Unless otherwise indicated, Scripture quotations are from The Holy Bible, English
Standard Version (ESV), copyright © 2001 by Crossway, a publishing ministry of
Good News Publishers. Used by permission. All rights reserved.

All rights reserved. Except as may be permitted by the Copyright Act, no part of
this publication may be reproduced in any form or by any means without prior
permission from the publisher.

J.D. Greear has asserted his right under the Copyright, Designs and Patents Act
1988 to be identified as author of this work.

Cover Design by Drew McCall

ISBN: 9781784988258 | Printed in Turkey

CONTENTS

ANNOUNCEMENT

What is Christianity, in a Sentence?

"For I am not ashamed of the gospel, for it is the power of God for salvation to everyone who believes..." (Romans 1:16)

For $1,111 an hour, Carissa Schumacher helps you connect with Jesus.

The fee purchases entry into Carissa's Los Angeles studio, where a gospel-style choir warms up the eclectic ensemble of enthusiastic enquirers—including a few megastars like Jennifer Aniston and Uma Thurman, both regulars at Sister Schumacher's.

When the singing ends, a hushed silence falls over the room, a keen sense of anticipation filling the air. Carissa enters dramatically, taking her seat before the crowd, where she sits quietly and stares out, just long enough to make you slightly uncomfortable.

And then, at long last, Jesus speaks through her. At least, according to Carissa that's what's happening. Carissa's Jesus prefers to go by "Yeshua"—which is not too strange, given that that was what his mom probably would have called him in Palestine 2,000 years ago. More curiously, her Jesus speaks with a British accent. (Evidently he understands that Americans grant you an automatic 15-IQ-point bonus if you wield the Queen's English.) Even to some of her followers, it all feels a bit strange. But yet they keep coming. One explained, "The Yeshua-channeling thing is way out there, and for some people, it's going to be insane, but... everything she's communicated to me just resonates."[1]

Resonates. In our age, that might be the most important word in evaluating spiritual experience. And an authentic spiritual experience is what so many of us are still looking for.

THAT UNSHAKABLE SPIRITUALITY

What strikes me about this story is not only that people pay $1,111 to spend an hour with Carissa's Yeshua, but that even in uber-secularized California—home of Silicon Valley, Hollywood, Stanford University, and U-Cal Berkeley—people are still seeking a connection with the divine.

After all, for more than a century, atheists have prophesied the coming of a brave, new world where belief in God is no longer necessary. Religious decline, they say, is the inevitable result of scientific progress, and soon religion will be enshrined in the museum of historical artifacts along with the sundial and the gasoline engine. The Beatles' John Lennon captured the growing consensus back in 1966 when he said, "Christianity will go. It will

---

1 "In Good Spirits"; https://www.nytimes.com/2021/11/26/style/carissa-schumacher-flamingo-estate-los-angeles.html (accessed July 7, 2022).

vanish and shrink. I needn't argue about that; I'm right and I will be proved right."

It's just that someone forgot to tell the Millennials.

Despite the best efforts of John Lennon, Ricky Gervais, and the New Atheists (Christopher Hitchens, Sam Harris, Richard Dawkins, and so on), Millennials and Gen Z-ers have just not been able to imagine there's no heaven. A recent *Washington Post* article notes that as knowledge of science has grown, religious fervor has grown right along with it.[2] That growth is not always reflected in "traditional" religious affiliations, but it's there and it's unmistakable. The future seems bright for religion: demographers predict, based on current trends, that the 21st century will be more religious than either the 19th or the 20th.

In that article, Jack Goldstone, a professor of public policy at George Mason University, concludes, "'Sociologists jumped the gun when they said the growth of modernization would bring a growth of secularization and unbelief. That is not what we're seeing ... People need religion."

The spiritual side of existence still resonates with us, even in our "secular" age.

---

2 "The world is expected to become more religious—not less," Sarah Pulliam Bailey, *The Washington Post*; April 24, 2015; https://www.washingtonpost.com/news/acts-of-faith/wp/2015/04/24/the-world-is-expected-to-become-more-religious-not-less/ (accessed July 7, 2022). See also "Religion is Dying? Don't Believe It": https://www.wsj.com/articles/religion-is-dying-dont-believe-it-nones-others-surveys-faith-institutions-atheists-agnostics-practice-minority-11659017037 (accessed September 5, 2022).

DECONSTRUCTION

What is *not* growing, however, is confidence in institutionalized religion. And so, growing side by side with our increasing thirst to engage with the spiritual is a movement called "deconstruction."

The basic idea behind deconstruction is that religious claims are often thinly-disguised power grabs—leaders leverage religious institutions to maintain power. And sadly there is plenty of evidence to support this theory: organized religion has been used to justify and perpetuate bigotry, slavery, systemic racism, misogyny, genocide, and many other societal evils.

Religion has proven, in fact, to be a quite potent political tool. The media now uses "Christian" and "Evangelical" primarily as political classifications. So it's hardly surprising that many assume that Christianity's primary function in our society is the protection and propagation of Western, white, suburban, middle-class values.

For others, Christianity is less about power or politics and is instead about personal fulfillment—in the end, it is little more than a self-help strategy, a way to become a better and more fulfilled you. Skim through the titles of the most popular Christian books of the last couple decades and you'll find ample evidence of this, too.

For these and many other reasons, deconstruction is not an altogether bad movement. It's hard to dispute the claims that religion has often been commandeered to serve the interests of the powerful, to further a political agenda, or to cater to the existential felt needs of the consumer.

Deconstruction's purpose, however, ought to be to recover the truth behind the artificial constructs. Deconstruction's goal cannot be to deconstruct *everything*. If everything is deconstructed, eventually you'll be left with nothing, and nothing is a great place for power-grabbing "strong men" to thrive. As C.S. Lewis said in his book *The Abolition of Man*, written in 1943:

> *"You cannot go on 'seeing through' things for ever. The whole point of seeing through something is to see something through it. It is good that the window should be transparent, because the street or garden beyond it is opaque ... a wholly transparent world is an invisible world. To 'see through' all things is the same as not to see."* [3]

In other words, the purpose of sweeping out the lies is to get to the truth. Healthy deconstruction means separating truth from the unhealthy, artificial constructs that so often surround it.

Now, in saying that, I certainly don't mean to imply that every religious institution is corrupt. Full disclosure: I'm a pastor, and so I lead a "Christian institution." I just want to acknowledge that some of the energy behind the deconstruction movement is legitimate, and that our institutions have sometimes been an impediment to truth rather than the conduits of it. Having run up against the shadow-side of such institutions, many truth-seekers have felt forced to look outside of them for authentic spirituality. Which leads us back to Carissa and her sessions offering you a connection with Jesus. All of us need something to make sense of life

---

3 *The Abolition of Man* (Oxford University Press, 1943).

and give it purpose. If you happen to have $1,111 in your wallet, why not spend it on finding something that works for you?

Here's why: in the end, we need more than spirituality that resonates; we need truth, because things that aren't real will eventually fail us.

Think of it as like trying to live on one of Jennifer's or Uma's studio sets. At a glance, the scenes they depict look so real—picture-perfect buildings, office spaces, living rooms, and greenery. The problem is that none of it is real. For a while, you can play-act like it is, but if you actually tried to live on a set, eventually you'd get pretty frustrated.

For something to sustain you for the long haul—throughout life and eternity—there has to be a reality behind the resonance.

So, before you empty out your bank account and head to LA, it's probably wise to take a beat. Carissa Schumacher's "Yeshua" may resonate, but is he real? For a thousand bucks an hour, are you encountering the real Jesus or just Carissa with a deeper voice?

With apologies to Jennifer and Uma: you're hearing from Carissa, not Christ.

But how do I know that?

Is there a way to know the difference between authentic and artificial spirituality?

And if institutions have failed you, is there a place you can still look to find truth?

If Carissa's sessions are not really Christianity, what is? And who gets to decide?

After all, Christianity sometimes has a "31 Flavors" feel. Conservative, liberal, Protestant, Catholic, Pentecostal, evangelical, non-denominational, high church, low church, Anglican, Baptist, etc., etc. If Christians can't even agree among themselves on what Christianity is, how can you be expected to know which version is "correct"? Where should you start in your quest for authentic spiritual experience?

I want to help you navigate those questions, in a book organized not around my thoughts, insights, and experiences but around what the architects of Christianity said about it. A book about Christian essentials, back before all the institutions, hierarchies, protocols, and politics. What the Bible-writer Jude called "the faith that was once for all delivered to the saints" (Jude 3): The core. The essence. For those first Christians, the Christian faith was not a philosophy or an experience that merely "worked for them." It *did* work for them—it made sense of life, and gave purpose in life, and gave peace about eternity—but the reason it worked was *because it was true*.

To access that core—that *Essential Christianity*—there is no better source than a letter that the early-church leader, or apostle, Paul, wrote to the first church in Rome.

PAUL'S LETTER TO ROME AS ESSENTIAL CHRISTIANITY

This book is not a commentary on Paul's letter to the Romans. Instead, it uses the major talking points of Paul's letter to construct a framework of Christian essentials. I'm asking, "If Paul were writing the book of Romans today, to people living in a 21st-century Western post-Christian culture rather than people living in a 1st-century Roman and Jewish culture, how would he write it?"

There are multiple reasons why I chose this approach. For one, throughout church history, Paul's letter to the Romans has been regarded as the clearest, purest, most in-depth explanation of Christian basics ever penned. Paul writes this letter to his highly cultured, well-educated friends in Rome, trying to explain why he's willing to stake his whole life on its truth.

Second, study of this letter has led to almost every Christian renewal in history. Back in the 4th century Augustine of Hippo, who is commonly regarded as one of the church's most important theologians, was transformed by one verse in Romans.[4] He later said that through his study of Romans, "all the shadows of doubt were dispelled." The 16th-century Protestant Reformer Martin Luther said that in Romans we find the "most important piece of the New Testament," the doctrine on which the church "rises or falls," and it was his exposition of Romans that led to the Protestant Reformation and the modern mission movement.

Third, Paul's logic in this book is so meticulous that, for its first 100 years or so, Harvard Law School required its first-year students to work their way through Romans to see how Paul built an argument, anticipating and answering objections along the way. In systematic fashion, Paul shows the coherence and reasonableness of the Christian message, setting it apart in the vast marketplace of spiritual ideas. It's amazing how often

---

4 Romans 13:14: "But put on the Lord Jesus Christ, and make no provision for the flesh, to gratify its desires."

you'll think of an objection to what Paul is saying and then find that in the next verse he starts answering it.

Finally, I believe Paul's line of reasoning in Romans is (as a non-Christian friend of mine told me recently) "surprisingly relevant" for those who aren't sure about Christianity. After all, Paul himself started out as a hardcore skeptic—the idea of the resurrection of Jesus was just as outrageous to him as it might be to you.

It may seem like a wild notion for you to consider that a 1st-century writer can meaningfully speak to your 21st-century questions and problems. But, if nothing else, Romans proves (to quote my seeking, not-yet-believing friend again) that "the fundamental anxieties and questions of the human condition have not changed in 2,000 years."

THE GOSPEL: FUEL FOR TIRED CHRISTIANS, TOO

If you are already a Christian, please don't see this book as something only for non-Christians. After all, Paul's primary audience in Romans is *Christians*: "all those ... called to be saints" (Romans 1:7). The gospel, he explains, is not just how we *begin* the Christian life; it's also how we *grow in* the Christian life.

Quite often I talk to Christians who feel weary and dry in their spiritual experience—tired of plodding along through all the rituals and forms that make for the supposedly faithful Christian life; tired of the division and politicking they see. Maybe that's you. You have no problem with consenting to the facts of the gospel, but your experience with it seems to be missing something. In Romans, the apostle Paul shows us how to experience the gospel as power *now*—power in our trials, doubts, struggles, and questions.

The gospel is not just the diving board off which we jump into Christianity—it's the swimming pool in which we swim. See this book as your invitation to rediscover the goodness, the excitement, the liberation, and the power of the Christian life. That's how Paul meant it for the church at Rome.

It's like Martin Luther said: "Any progress in the Christian life comes from beginning again"—by going back to the gospel.

WHAT IS THE GOSPEL?

"Gospel" is one of those words that Christians often use but rarely define, but it's basically shorthand for the essential Christian message. Today, that word has almost exclusively religious connotations, but when Jesus and the apostles first started using it, it wasn't a religious word at all. If an emperor won a great battle, for example, he would send heralds out with a "gospel" (literally, "good news") about his victory. "I have good news," the herald proclaimed: "Our emperor has won for us a great battle— we no longer need to live in fear." Early Christians commandeered that word to encapsulate what Jesus had done. Our King has won a battle for us, and now we are invited to join in his victory and rest in his peace.

This gospel announcement is the heart of Christianity. We can get a lot of other things wrong, but if we get the gospel right, we have Christianity. Without it, whatever we have (no matter how much it resonates), we don't.

So what is this gospel announcement?

Paul starts off Romans with this short explanation. The gospel is the good news about...

• who Jesus is

• what he's done

• what he brings[5]

That's how he organizes the book of Romans. Based on that, here's a workable definition we can use, then, from this point forward:

> God, in an act of grace, sent his Son, Jesus, to earth as a man so that through his life, death, and resurrection he could rescue us, reign as King, and lead us into the eternal, full life we were created to enjoy.

Let's briefly break that down.

God...

The gospel begins with God. God exists, and he's been moving and speaking throughout history. That's already a big claim, and we're only one word in! How can we know he's there? What is he like? How do we know when he's speaking to us? We'll come back to that in chapter 2.

... in an act of grace...

That word "grace" means "undeserved kindness." Grace, properly understood, is what makes Christianity different from every other spiritual approach. Grace is the entire

---

5 He's the "Son of God in power" (Romans 1:4). He's defeated death for us by dying under our curse and rising again (Romans chapters 3, 5, and 6). He brings a new creation in which former enemies are reconciled, friends live in love, and peace reigns (chapters 12 – 16). Thanks to Michael Bird for this helpful breakdown.

basis of the gospel: the melody line around which all other Christian truths are played.

C.S. Lewis, the author of the acclaimed Chronicles of Narnia, was also an Oxford University professor and a convinced atheist who became a Christian in his thirties. One afternoon he was walking through the corridors of Oxford when he heard someone call his name from inside a classroom. A group of his colleagues were gathered in a lecture room, listing out on a blackboard all the things world religions have in common—things like morality, accountability, judgment, worship. Knowing that Lewis was a Christian, they challenged him: "Jack (that was his nickname—I have no idea how you get from Clive Staples to Jack), tell us what Christianity believes that is not already listed on this blackboard." Lewis went in, looked at their list for a moment, walked up to the board, took a piece of chalk, and wrote just one simple word:

"Grace."

Lewis put down the chalk and walked out without a word. That's an Oxford don's version of a mic drop. Two things to learn from that story: one, never try to outwit C.S. Lewis. Two, grace is what distinguishes Christianity from every other religion. Christianity, at its core, is not good advice about what we must go and do for God, but rather, good news about what he's done for us. It's not primarily instructions in morality or accountability or goodness but a declaration of grace.

... *sent his Son, Jesus...*

Or, as the apostle John explains it, God himself became a man and dwelt among us (John 1:14). More on the what and why of this later.

... so that he could rescue us...

The most important thing about Jesus is not what he taught but what he did. Paul's letter to the Romans, in fact, speaks very little about what Jesus taught and a whole lot about what he did. It's not what he taught that saved us, but what he did. The symbol of Christianity is not a lectern but a cross.

Christianity is, in its essence, a rescue religion. Which, of course, raises the questions: Why do we need rescuing? And how can a man who lived 2,000 years ago have done something then that can rescue me today? Great questions. That's chapters 3 to 6 of this book.

... reign as King, and lead us into the eternal, full life we were created to enjoy.

The gospel is not just about what Jesus came to rescue you from, but what he came to rescue you for: the full, eternal life that we were created to enjoy. As Paul explains, the gospel restores us to the life we were made for all along (the subject of chapters 7 to 10). This is what a lot of Christians, as well as non-believers, forget, but it pulsates through almost every chapter of Paul's great letter.

IT RESONATES BECAUSE IT'S REAL

Paul presents these truths not merely as insights that resonate but as realities that are, well, real. In fact, the reason they resonate is because they are real.

That doesn't mean they always come easily or instinctively. Some of what Paul says about the gospel you might find quite offensive. I certainly have.

That was Paul's experience too. He did not start out his adult life as a Christian—quite the contrary. He was the church's fiercest persecutor—he believed Christians were too forgiving of moral lawbreakers and not angry enough about Roman occupation. And yet, one afternoon on a dusty road to the city of Damascus, Paul encountered a power unlike anything he'd ever experienced. He experienced the resurrected Jesus, and in that moment Jesus transformed his life.[6]

It is this power that, he says, he is now "eager" to tell us about (Romans 1:15).

Are you open to what God says, even if it surprises, confronts, and, at times, angers you?

I hope that you are. I suspect that's why you picked up this book. And here's the good news—it won't cost you $1,111 an hour to read it.

---

6 You can read what happened in Acts 9:1-19.

UNDENIABLE

How Do We Even Know There's a God?

"For his invisible attributes ... have been clearly perceived ... in the things that have been made."
(Romans 1:20)

So there I was, sitting in one of the happiest places on earth, about to feast upon the nectar of the gods: a Waffle House chocolate-chip waffle and hash browns scattered, smothered, covered, chunked, topped, diced, and peppered. (For those of you not from the American Southeast, we consider the Waffle House to be our greatest contribution to cultural progress and the pinnacle of human flourishing.) That was when I overheard a conversation between a waitress and the guy in the booth next to me that was the last thing I was expecting to hear in a Waffle House.

The man said, "Yeah, but the *most* important question in life is who *God* is."

Then he continued, "The problem, though, is knowing *what* to believe about God—if he's even there. There are so many different opinions—how are we supposed to know which one is right?"

And there I was, my mouth full of hash browns, thinking, "You people are so in luck. I have my Master of Divinity. This is my kind of discussion." (For the record, I've always thought that saying one has "mastered" divinity seems a bit of stretch.) I waved my hand to interject myself into the conversation. Thankfully, before anyone noticed me, I heard the waitress respond...

"Yeah... but you know who I absolutely despise? Them 'born-again' types. When they come in here and start talking about God, it's not a conversation anymore. They don't care about you; all they care about is showing why they are right."

Then she saw my hand raised, and she said, "Can I help you?"

I sized up the situation, took a deep breath, and said...

"Yeah... I just needed a refill on my tea."

I am a born-again Christian, and in this chapter I don't want to fulfill her (or anyone else's!) stereotypes. I just think my waitress friend (I got to know her later and we had some great conversations) and the guy she was speaking with had raised an important question:

What can we know about God? And how can we know that we know it?

I'm not sure with whom you empathize most in that story. Maybe it's the guy, knowing that this question about God is an important one. Or maybe it's the waitress, tired of Christians who seem more interested in winning arguments and scoring points than actual reflective conversation. Or maybe it's me, quietly drinking my tea and wondering how I got caught in the middle of all this.

But now imagine a fourth person is listening in from the other side of the restaurant. It's Paul, a man both quicker in thought and greater in courage than me. I wonder, what would he have said if he'd been in Waffle House that day finishing up his hash browns? I imagine him saying, *I'm so glad you asked. That's a great question. Mind if I take a run at it?*

GOD HAS MADE HIMSELF KNOWN

"What can be known about God is plain to them, because God has shown it to them. For his invisible attributes, namely, his eternal power and divine nature, have been clearly seen since the creation of the world, being understood through what he has made."
(Romans 1:19-20)

Paul (as is his habit) packs a lot into a couple sentences. Here's his basic claim: God has made the basic truths about himself known to every person who's ever lived. He's left his fingerprints in various places, if we have eyes to see them.

Philosophers helpfully grouped these fingerprints into four primary categories, and then unhelpfully gave them complicated names. I'm going to use those complicated names, but don't let them trip you up. The concepts are pretty simple. I figure if we can memorize the name of our $14, 16-ingredient drink at Starbucks, we can learn these. And, if you happen to find yourself in a philosophical discussion about the nature of God at the Waffle House late one afternoon and drop in one of these multisyllabic masterpieces, it's sure to increase your standing in the debate.

These are four ways that the apostle says God reveals himself in creation:

1. The Cosmological Fingerprint

One of the things that creation makes plain, Paul says, is God's "eternal power and divine nature."

It goes back to the most basic question of all: *why is there something rather than nothing?* And given that there is something, where did that original something come from? Even if you believe that the Big Bang accounts for the complexity of everything we see, what caused the Big Bang? Few things are more obvious than "nothing times nobody can't equal everything." Zero times zero always ends up as zero, never the Alcyoneus galaxy or the human DNA cell.

The late atheist thinker Carl Sagan was once interviewed on a radio program, explaining how everything in the universe could be accounted for by an explosion of matter at the center of the known universe billions and billions of years ago. "And where did the materials that went into this explosion come from?" the interviewer asked. "That's precisely where science stops," he responded.

That leaves me feeling... well, dissatisfied—because that might be the most important question of them all. Even if the theory of evolution could explain all the complexity and beauty and mystery of human experience, I still find myself unable to explain how nothing multiplied by nobody really *could* account for everything. And it feels unfair to say that this one question—where it all came from—has to be accepted as a mystery for which science has no answer.

Even the most popular atheist of our generation, Richard Dawkins, accepts that getting from infinite nothingness to the Big Bang takes a leap of faith:

> *"Any honest quest for truth must … explain such monstrosities of improbability as a rainforest, a coral reef, or a universe … The [explanation] doesn't have to be natural selection. Admittedly, nobody has ever thought of a better one. But there could be others yet to be discovered."* [7]

In other words, Dawkins acknowledges that while he thinks Darwin's theory of evolution works for biology, he knows it has no answer for cosmology (ultimate origins). Cosmology is still, in a sense, waiting on its Darwin, he says.[8] He thinks he has a pretty good idea how primordial materials evolved into life but admits he has no idea where those materials came from. And yet, he remains confident that one day we'll figure that out. Most would call that a blind leap of faith.

Paul's answer is that everything came from God. Something *must* be eternal—we can't go back in infinite regress forever—and that "eternal" thing has to either be something physical or something metaphysical (that is, divine). Neither can be *proven*, per se—but is it more reasonable to believe that matter is eternal or that God is? Is it even possible for something physical to exist eternally? The fact that there is something rather than nothing suggests an eternal, metaphysical designer behind

---

7 Using the imagery of "cranes" as a mechanism for understanding the universe's origins, Dawkins candidly admits that we are still in search of "a cosmological crane to stand alongside Darwin's biological one." *The God Delusion*, (Houghton Mifflin, 2008), p 185.

8 As above.

it, at some point, even if we're unsure of the mechanisms that that deity used to make it all happen.

The point is that you don't walk up to a work of art, like the Sistine Chapel, the Taj Mahal, or the works of Shakespeare, and assume they are the lucky outcome of a fortuitous accident. You assume, instinctively, that there is a designer. It's the same when you take a walk in creation. It feels like a work of art, not an accident. It points us toward an Artist.

2. The Teleological Fingerprint

Telos means purpose. This "argument" takes its name from the fact that there appears to be a purpose to the cosmos. Our cosmos at least *looks* like it was designed: and more than that, like it was designed *for us*.

Ecologists, for example, note the extremely delicate nature of our ecosystem. They say that, for one, if the level of oxygen in the air dropped by just 6%, we would all suffocate and die. If it rose by 4%, our planet would erupt into a giant fireball, causing us all to die in a vortex of flames. Even more harrowingly, if the carbon dioxide level in the atmosphere were even 0.5% higher—our world would become an oven, and if it were 0.02% lower, we would have no atmosphere at all. More death.

Or take our position in the solar system. Cosmologists say that if the earth were 2% closer to the sun, it would be too hot for water to exist. And if our planet were not tilted at exactly 23.5 degrees, temperatures would be far more extreme, so extreme that—you guessed it—we'd all die. Or if Jupiter were not the size it is in the place that is, there would be around 10,000 the number of asteroids hitting earth than happens now, and—right again—we'd all die. (Let's all pause for a silent moment of appreciation for Jupiter.) As one author, reflecting on these remarkable "coincidences" in our solar system, put it, "Our existence seems to be not merely a virtually impossible miracle but the most outrageous miracle conceivable."[9] The Oxford University mathematician John Lennox said that the survival of our ecosystem is like a marksman hitting a coin "at the far side of the observable universe, twenty billion light years away."[10] Randomly arriving at the right cosmological conditions for life on earth to thrive would be something like tossing 30 razor blades into the air, having them all land edge on edge—and then adding something like an elephant on top.

If you put down your telescope and pull out a microscope, again you'll find the same mind-boggling complexity on the molecular level. Even the most basic DNA strands are incredibly complex—enough so that Francis Collins, the head of the human genome project (who is himself a Christian), says, "How could a cosmic accident ever result in something of the digital elegance of a DNA strand?"[11] It's like thinking that an explosion in an ink factory could inadvertently produce the collected works of Shakespeare. And here's the late Stephen Hawking (not a Christian), probably the world's most famous scientist since Albert Einstein, on the way atoms are constructed:

---

9   Eric Metaxas, *Miracles* (Penguin, 2014), p 54.

10 *God's Undertaker*, excerpt retrieved at http://www.focus.org.uk/lennox.php (accessed July 11, 2022).

11 "DNA, with its phosphate-sugar backbone and intricately arranged organic bases, stacked neatly on top of one another and paired together at each rung of the twisted double helix, seems an utterly improbable molecule to have 'just happened'—especially since DNA seems to possess no intrinsic means of copying itself." Francis Collins, *The Language of God: A Scientist Presents Evidence for Belief* (Free Press, 2006), p 91.

"The laws of science, as we know them, at present contain many precise ratios, like the size of the electric charge of electrons and the ratio of the masses of the proton and the electron. The remarkable fact is that the values of these numbers seem to have been very finely adjusted to make possible the development of life." To return to a familiar theme, if the proton and electron did not have *exactly* opposite charge values (charges calibrated independently of each other), atoms would not hold together and... well, we'd never have been around to die.

Scientists sometimes refer to this as the "Goldilocks principle." Our universe is "just right" for us to survive. Make the smallest tweak and none of us exist.

Now, maybe you say, "Well, we're just lucky. We just happen to be in that one-in-a-trillion-trillion solar system where everything came together just right." Is that possible? Mathematicians might say yes. The odds might be incredibly small, but they are there. Think of it like this: the odds of tossing a coin and having it come up heads 1,000 times in a row is infinitesimally small. But if you had 1,000,000,000 people lined up, each tossing a coin once every second for the next 10 trillion years, eventually one might get that "1,000 in a row" streak. Well, we just happen to be in that one-in-a-trillion-trillion solar system where everything came together. Given enough time, eventually things came together just right, and the result is us, marveling at how incredibly lucky we are.

Some scientists say even then it wouldn't be possible, given realities like "irreducible complexity" and other factors that make random, blind forces incapable of the design inherent in our bodies and our ecosystem, no matter how many trillions of years you gave it.

But instead of arguing about what's technically possible, perhaps it's more reasonable to focus on whether the simplest and most compelling explanation for what we see is that our planet is one big, incredibly lucky accident that we just happen to be around to observe. It seems to me that to arrive at that conclusion requires a compelling reason to *want* to believe that. And Paul says some of us have just such a reason... but I'm getting ahead of myself. More on that in the next chapter.

3. The Moral Fingerprint

All of us have a voice within that talks to us about how we ought to live. "Right" and "wrong" are categories that we understand (even if we disagree on what goes in which category), and we tend to feel guilty for failing to live up to whatever we believe is right. This feeling is pervasive in every human culture on earth. Paul calls this phenomenon "the law written on our hearts" (Romans 2:15). Even in places without the Bible, he's arguing, God has seared the basic shape of his law into our consciences.

It is, I think, implausible that this moral sense would have evolved in our species through the survival-of-the-fittest mechanism that evolution demands—that is to say, that our morality is really a self-preservation instinct which we pass on to our offspring and that masquerades as a virtue.

For one thing, while a sense of right and wrong and feelings of guilt for failing to live up to what's right are pervasive in human culture, they're absent from the animal kingdom. You've never found your cat sniffling under the bed after he cruelly played with a mouse for a while before he ate it, thinking, "I've got to stop doing this." Yes, I'm aware that Bruce the shark beats himself up in *Finding Nemo* for impulsively eating fish, reminding himself, "Fish are friends, not food. Fish are friends, not food." But that's Pixar fantasy, not the real world.

You and I have a moral compass that is found nowhere in the animal world. So where does it come from? "Survival of the fittest" can't satisfactorily explain it. If our species got here by beating out all other competing species, why should we privilege our species by saying any violence against us is wrong? That sounds like species-ism.

The Bible's answer is that our moral sense comes from the God who has set our world up with right and wrong and who has stamped his image on our hearts. That image is there whether we believe in him or not. Survival of the fittest may work as an explanation for why various traits of various species survive, but humans have proven quite uncomfortable with survival of the fittest as the basis for a code of ethics. There is something in us that knows, for instance, that sexually molesting a powerless child is not just *disadvantageous* for species propagation, it's also *evil*.

4. The Desire Fingerprint

Quite simply, we find in ourselves yearnings for things beyond the material world. We long for love. To matter. For significance. We don't like the idea that one day we will simply cease to exist.

Walter Isaacson wrote the definitive biography of the iconic Apple co-founder, Steve Jobs. According to Isaacson, Jobs, a self-proclaimed Buddhist, began questioning the meaning of life and the idea of God in the few months before his death.

"I remember sitting in his backyard in his garden one day and he started talking about God," recalled Isaacson.

> "He said, 'Sometimes I believe in God, sometimes I don't. I think it's 50-50 maybe. But ever since I've had cancer, I've been thinking about it more. And I find myself believing a bit more. I kind of—maybe it's cause I want to believe in an afterlife. That when you die, it doesn't just all disappear. The wisdom you've accumulated. Somehow it lives on.'
>
> "Then [Isaacson continued] he paused for a second and he said, 'Yeah, but sometimes I think it's just like an on-off switch. Click and you're gone.' He paused again, and he said, 'And that's why I don't like putting on-off switches on Apple devices.'" [12]

There's a reason why Jobs felt that way. There's a reason why we all do. It's because God has pressed his fingerprint—his eternal power and divine nature—into our souls.

It is impossible to improve here on the words of C.S. Lewis:

> "Creatures are not born with desires unless satisfaction for those desires exists. A baby feels hunger: well, there is such a thing as food. A duckling wants to swim: well, there is such a thing as water. Men feel sexual desire: well, there is such a thing as sex. If I find in myself a desire which no experience in this world can satisfy, the most probable explanation is that I was made for another world. If none of my earthly pleasures satisfy it, that does not prove that

---

12 "Steve Jobs biography reveals his struggle with religion, faith in God," https://christiantoday.com.au/news/steve-jobs-biographer-reveals-his-struggle-with-religion-faith-in-god.html (accessed September 19, 2022).

the universe is a fraud. Probably earthly pleasures were never meant to satisfy it, but only to arouse it, to suggest the real thing." [13]

Atheism says to these desires, "Too bad. Toughen up, buttercup. Embrace your aloneness in the universe. Be brave." The philosopher Albert Camus, one of the 20th century's most famous atheists, called this "the absurdity of life": "In a universe without God, we only have the conscious certainty of death without hope," he wrote. To him, life was one long, tragic comedy in which we search for a meaning that just. isn't. there.

If, on the other hand, there is a God who is full of love and who made us to know and enjoy him forever, then our desires for love, meaning, and hope make sense. These feelings are not absurd—they're pointers to the existence of a God who created us for those things.

In 2009, A.N. Wilson, the British journalist, biographer, and thinker, a big voice in the philosophical world, put it this way: "Atheism has no answer whatsoever to the question of how [this animated sack of accidental chemicals—you, and me] could be capable of love or heroism or poetry."

No love, no heroism, no poetry. This is a pretty significant deficit. Just imagine an honest atheistic Hallmark Valentine's card: "My genes have determined that you are useful for the propagation of my DNA, and my synapses are so ordered as to incline me to think that being with you would create in me serene and titillating feelings that I am bound to enjoy and mistake for actual self-emptying love. So, um, let's copulate?"

---

13 *Mere Christianity* (Macmillan, 1952), p 120.

Doesn't quite have the same romantic zing to it, does it?

We don't live like that because instinctively we understand that life is about more than that.

ECHOES AND FINGERPRINTS, NOT PROOFS

I am not saying that these are *proofs* of God, but rather evidences of his existence—divine fingerprints. Sure, a fingerprint can be forged, but you'd need a compelling reason to believe it was forged before you wrote it off. In Romans 1, Paul is not so much concerned with building out logical proofs of God as he is pointing us to divine fingerprints which should be easy to recognize and reasonable to accept. Think of it this way: if I get home and find a note on the table in my wife's handwriting that reads, "Happy Birthday, sweetheart. Meet me at the Waffle House," and then she signs it with that special name that I have for her that only I know, it is *possible* it is an elaborate ruse by a conman to lure me out of the house so he can rob me, and that he's mimicked her handwriting exactly and has luckily guessed her special pet name for me. Given enough robbers in enough neighborhoods, one could get lucky enough to pull that off. But is that the *most likely* explanation for the note?

Paul's point is that it takes an *agenda* not to hear the voice of God speaking in creation, because the voice is sufficiently clear: "What can be known about God is evident [that is, there is evidence] among them, because God has shown it to them. For his invisible attributes, that is, his eternal power and divine nature, have been clearly seen since the creation of the world, being understood through what he has made." There is enough evidence out there in the cosmos and in here in me that we can reasonably recognize that a Creator is behind it all. Paul is so sure of this that he goes so far as to say that people who do not believe in God are "without excuse."

But, in that case, Paul has a problem, statistically speaking.

You see, if there were 40 people in Waffle House that morning, about 10 of them likely would have been atheists or agnostics. And if we'd been dining in the UK, on average over 15 of them would have confidently argued over their bacon and eggs, beans, black pudding, and fried bread (an American's interpretation of a typical British breakfast) that there is no God.

So, here's the question: If the existence of God is so "evident" from the fact that the world *is,* from the *way* the world is, and from the way *we* are, then why are there so many intelligent, thoughtful, considered, well-read *atheists*? And why do so many who think he's there sometimes feel unsure of it?"

In other words, if the evidence is so compelling, why are some not persuaded by it?

Good questions. We're probably going to need another round of waffles.

REFUSAL

If God Is Real, Why Doesn't Everybody Believe in Him?

"Since they did not see fit to acknowledge God..."
(Romans 1:28)

Something isn't right with the world. I've never met anyone who wouldn't agree to that. We lock our doors, and we teach our kids about dangerous people. People treat each other unkindly. Why?

Why is our world such a mess? What's the root issue? Maybe you think the problem is a lack of education. Or the presence of classism. Or systemic racism. Or the breakdown of the family structure. Or maybe you think it's just a handful of bad apples poisoning the whole lot, and they need to be jailed. Maybe you think religion is the problem. Maybe it's all of the above.

In our more reflective moments, most of us recognize that something isn't right *inside of us* too. I'm embarrassed by many of the thoughts and feelings that go through my own heart. Have you ever had one of those moments where something slipped out of your mouth that totally embarrassed you? An outburst of anger, something snippy and unfair about someone, a demeaning joke, or the verbalization of a lust. Later, when you feel bad about what you said, and you go back to the person to apologize, what do you say to them? "I'm sorry. I didn't mean that. *That's not really me.*"

Hmmm. But in the moment, it felt like you. In the moment you said it, *you meant it.* It came out quite naturally. And if it's not really *you*, then where exactly did it come from?

Maybe a better explanation is that as we grow up, we get better at filtering some of what is down there, so it doesn't come out and embarrass us. But just because we don't *verbalize* something doesn't mean it isn't *inside* us. The real, unfiltered us is usually not very pretty.

Or think of it this way: how would you like it if there were someone who, whenever they wanted, could just read whatever you were thinking? Imagine if someone developed an app so that whatever came into your mind displayed on their screen. How awful would that be? Recently, I rented a car that had a new GPS feature on it: every time you went over the speed limit, a pleasant (but slightly alarmed) little voice would announce the correct speed limit—"The speed limit is 55"—to everyone in the car. I felt judged and embarrassed. But it made me think about how uncomfortable it would be if a little voice announced to bystanders every time something came up in my heart that shouldn't be there. I'd be sitting in a restaurant looking at the dessert menu, and the little voice would announce, "You are already 12 lbs. overweight." I'd be walking through the mall as a woman walked by, and the little voice would say, "*Your* wife's name is Veronica, and that's not her."

My point is that we know, deep down, that there are not only problems in the world and with other people; there are problems with *us*, too.

The pastor Andy Stanley points out that we like to call dumb decisions that we make "mistakes." "I made some *mistakes* in my previous marriage." "I made some *mistakes* at my former job." Or when a politician or celebrity is discovered to have been involved in a multi-year affair, they refer to those recurring rendezvous as "poor choices" or "mistakes."

But does "mistake" really capture the magnitude of an affair? Their spouse usually doesn't think so. Neither do their kids. A mistake is what happens when you forget to carry the 1 in a math problem. Offended spouses feel something different; they feel betrayed.

We need a better word than "mistake," because "mistake" just doesn't cover it. And that's where Paul turns next. He explains that there is a disease that afflicts all of us, and the location of that disease is square in the middle of our hearts. It's a word that hardly anyone likes anymore, but there's no getting around it. Three simple letters, big massive meaning: sin.

According to Paul, the presence of sin determines what we perceive about God and how we respond to him. Let's consider what Paul teaches about this problem in our hearts. What is sin?

THE "I" PROBLEM

In 1543, Nicholas Copernicus turned the astronomical word upside down. Previously, astronomers had assumed that the earth was at the center of the universe and that everything else revolved around it. It made sense—every day and night the sun, moon and celestial bodies passed in front of us for our enjoyment. Then Copernicus discovered the groundbreaking truth about our solar system: the earth, as well as all the other planets, revolves around the sun. We're not the center. And that's a good thing.

Pre-Copernican astronomy is a pretty good metaphor for humanity today. We live as though everything else revolves around us. Our primary concern with whatever comes into our lives is how it affects us. If our lives were a movie with a main character, that main character would be us.

Even if we "get religious," we think mostly about how God fits into *our* life stories. We want to figure out what we need to do to get him orbiting us so that we get the blessings of his presence. You could summarize the collective prayer requests of most religious people in the world this way: "God, this is what I need. God, bless this, fix that, smite him. God, you didn't do this, so I'm mad at you. In fact, disappoint me again and I will punish you by not believing in you."

Paul describes humanity like this: "For although they knew God, they did not honor him as God or give thanks to him" (Romans 1:21). We didn't want God to be the center; *we* wanted to be the center. We didn't want him to make the rules; *we* wanted to make them. We didn't want to devote our lives to his glory; we wanted him (and everybody else) to devote himself to *ours*. We didn't want to acknowledge God as the source of all our blessing; we wanted to take credit for who we've become and what we've accomplished. We became cosmic plagiarizers, ignoring God's role in our lives and taking all the credit as our own. We live as if our talents, our brains, our energy, and our every breath somehow originated with us. We assume that we know best, that our way is the right way, and that our feelings on an issue are the supreme authority.

This is what the Bible calls "sin." Sin is not so much an action as an attitude—a displacement of God at the center with ourselves.

I always told my kids that they could understand sin by how it's spelled: S-I-N. Sin happens when I put myself at the center of everything. It's the big "I" problem.

Ultimately, self-worship and self-will were original sins that led to all the others. It is the desire for "I" to be in the center that Paul says causes us to "suppress the truth" (v 18) about the God who created us and to whom we owe absolute allegiance.

THE IDOL PROBLEM

After we swapped out God for ourselves as the center of our lives, we turned to things he'd created as replacements for him. The human heart needs something to orbit, something to live for, something to assign ultimate value to. No longer wanting God to occupy that spot, we turned to other things, created things (Romans 1:25).

One of the Hebrew words for worship is "*kabod*" (often translated into English as "glory"). It means, literally, "to give weight to." We worship whatever we give the most weight to. What carries the most weight in your life?

Ask yourself:

- If I could change one thing about my life right now, what would it be?

- What am I willing to make great sacrifices for in order to obtain? (Sacrifice and worship always go hand in hand.)

- What do I worry most about never obtaining? Or, what do I have right now that I most worry about losing?

The things that come to mind when asked those questions are what have the most *kabod* in our hearts. We give them "glory." In a way, we worship them because we couldn't imagine life being good without them. We have to have them, at all costs. The Bible calls these things our "idols."

Maybe it's the approval of people. Or the love of your family. A thriving career. A healthy bank balance. Exhilarating romance. Power, comfort, or control. What makes an idol bad is not what it is in itself but the weight we give it in our hearts. Idols are not usually bad things in themselves. An idol is a *good thing* we give the weight of a *God thing,* which makes it a *bad thing.*

For me, one of my idols has always been the approval of people. In high school, I wore what my friends told me I should wear, talked the way they thought I should talk, and acted like they thought I should act so that they would approve of me. I realize now that I spent my entire high-school career trying to please a bunch of people I didn't even really like! Even now, I often find myself desperate for others' praise and devastated by their criticism.

Our propensity to worship is not something noted merely by preachers and theologians. A few years ago the acclaimed postmodern novelist David Foster Wallace, who was himself an atheist, said this at a commencement speech at Kenyon University:

> "In the day-to day trenches of adult life, there is actually no such thing as atheism. There is no such thing as not worshiping. Everybody worships. The only choice we get is what to worship." [14]

You can no more turn off your drive for worship by not being "religious" than you can turn off your sex drive by remaining celibate. The question is not *if* you worship something, but *what* you worship.

Or consider the words of Ernest Becker, a Jewish agnostic, in his Pulitzer Prize-winning book, *The Denial of Death*:

> "Modern man edged himself into an impossible situation. If he no longer had God, how was he to [find meaning, to know that he mattered]? One of the first ways that occurred to him ... was the 'romantic solution' ... The love partner becomes the divine ideal within which to fulfill one's life ... Spirituality, which once referred to another dimension of things, is now brought down to this earth and given form in another individual human being ... In case we are inclined to forget how deified the romantic love object is, the popular songs continually remind us ... In one word, the love object is God." [15]

Becker wrote that in 1973, but our songs today point to the same thing: "You're the meaning in my life, the inspiration; you brought me to life, you're my missing puzzle piece. With you I'm complete... I'd rather die without a you and I." (A musical mash-up from Chicago,

---

14 https://fs.blog/david-foster-wallace-this-is-water/ (accessed September 16, 2022).
15 *The Denial of Death* (The Free Press, 1973), p 167-168.

Katy Perry, and Lady Gaga.) One thing all humans have in common, Paul says, is this: we have all chosen something to worship in place of God.

OUR WORLD UNRAVELS

What is God's response to our idolatrous worship? The Bible's answer is surprising. He first says, *As you wish.*

Paul says that God "gave [us] up" to our idols (see Romans 1:24, 26, 28). Essentially, he said to us, *If you think you want a world without me, I will let you experience a taste of it.*

It's what we asked for, but it turns out not to be what we expected. Our rejection of God left our world in chaos. Because God alone possesses infinite glory and goodness, our lives only work with him at the center.

Let's go back to Copernicus for a minute. Astronomers say it's a good thing that the sun is at the center of our solar system. If not, we wouldn't *have* a solar system. The sun is the only celestial body in our solar system with the gravitational power to keep everything else in orbit. Imagine that the earth decides that it wants to be at the center; that way it gets all the attention. The problem is, at 1/30,000th the size of the sun, the earth doesn't have the gravitational power to keep everything in place. If the sun were angry about being displaced from the center, it wouldn't have to send out a blast of nuclear energy to discipline the earth—it could just let things play out naturally. Everything would simply unravel. The sun would experience no difference, but life on earth would end.

We refused to say to God, "Thy will be done," and God said to us, *Ok, then THY will be done.* And then everything started to come apart. This is what Paul means when he says, "The wrath [the settled anger] of God is revealed [that is, *is being* revealed] from heaven against all ungodliness and unrighteousness of [people], who by their unrighteousness suppress the truth" (v 18). We are right now getting a taste of a world without God. Which leads us back to the one thing we can all agree on: something is desperately wrong with our world. It's as the British philosopher G.K. Chesterton said: the depth of human sinfulness is the one Christian doctrine that is empirically verifiable. Just look around.

Actually, we don't even need to look around. We just need to look inside—because removing God from the center corrupted us from top to bottom. Paul includes a list of specific ways in which idolatry corrupted us: covetousness, malice, envy, murder, strife, sexual perversion, deceit, gossip, slandering, boastfulness, disobeying parents, unfaithfulness, ruthlessness (v 26-31). And this is not intended to be an exhaustive list: it's just a sample. That list includes spiritual disorder, relational disorder, economic disorder, familial disorder, sexual disorder, and just about any other kind of disorder you can think of. Some things on that list will affect you more than others, but our decision to put ourselves at the center has corrupted us all. We may manifest that corruption in different ways, but the root disease is the same.

Ultimately, all these other disorders go back to a worship disorder. That was noted, again, by David Foster Wallace in that Kenyon College commencement address I quoted earlier:

> "[What] you worship will eat you alive. If you worship money and things, if they are where you tap real

meaning in life, then you will never have enough, never feel you have enough. It's the truth. Worship your body and beauty and sexual allure and you will always feel ugly. And when time and age start showing, you will die a million deaths before they finally grieve you."

It's this that makes life absurd—it's a tragedy, and we're the victims. But we're also the perpetrators because we chose this. Not only that, but in choosing to worship these things, we become the kind of people we weren't created to be and don't ourselves really want to be.

THE GOOD NEWS OF THE BAD NEWS

We asked to be in a world without God, and God gave us what we wanted. The ultimate end point of that trajectory of our choice to walk away from God is hell itself—the complete absence of God, and along with him his beauty, his gifts, and the hope, meaning, and joy that go along with them.

Paul talks of a "day of wrath when God's righteous judgment will be [fully] revealed" (2:5). That's "hell." You may only think of hell as a place where a wrathful God punishes sin, but what the first chapter of Romans shows us is that the door to hell is locked first from the inside. Hell is God granting us our primal request, "My will, not thine, be done!" Because the "earth" of our lives has rebelled against the "sun" of his presence, we're spiraling out of his gravitational pull into the darkness and the emptiness of the great abyss, with no light and no way back, all the while muttering, "Now I am free to be in charge! Now I am the center of my existence, I am the master of my fate, I am the captain of my soul," and wondering why it feels so cold and miserable. And tragically, it only gets worse: our descent ends in the black hole of hell.

None of this sounds like good news. But if you ask me, it's the best explanation for the beauty and tragedy of this mystery we call life. We're created by a good God to enjoy his good gifts, but we're spiraling away from him. And that sets us up for the good news.

Albert Camus said the only way to respond to the absurdity of life in a godless universe was to accept "the conscious certainty of death without hope." But, according to Paul, this is *not* a Godless universe—and that means that you can respond to the reality of your sin and God's judgment with hope—because of the gospel message: that in his grace God sent his Son, Jesus, to rescue people so they could enjoy life with him.

In judgment, God gives you what you ask for; but in the gospel, he offers you what you were created for and what inwardly you long for. The God who made you has come to rescue you. Creation points to the power of God. Your conscience testifies about the justice of God. The gospel now demonstrates for you the love of God.

A HEART ISSUE

Ah, but again, we're getting ahead of ourselves.

For now, I'm still sitting in Waffle House. Here is what I should have said (though it's taken us nearly two whole chapters, and my hash browns would be cold by now):

> "There is abundant evidence for the existence of God, but we suppress it because we think we want a world, a life, without God."

This means that the question "Is there even a God?" is one that we answer more with our hearts than our heads. The problem is not that the evidence is not there; it's that our hearts don't want to see it. The philosopher William James, who many regard as a forerunner to 20th-century postmodernism, said that in determining what we believe, more important than evidence is (to use the title of his most famous lecture) "The Will to Believe." What we believe, James explained, is less determined by the evidence itself than by what we want to believe. Postmodern philosophy patted itself on the back for this great discovery. And it was a great discovery. But Paul got there two millennia earlier:

> "For though they knew God, they did not honor him as God or give thanks to him, but they became futile in their thinking, and their foolish hearts were darkened."
> (Romans 1:21)

In other words, our heads are controlled by our hearts. It wasn't that we *couldn't* figure out the truth about God; we didn't *want* to figure it out because we didn't really *want* to know it. The flaw was not in the evidence but in the hearts considering that evidence.

So *denial* of God's existence, according to Paul, is not the faulty conclusion of a genuinely confused mind but the subconscious desire of a heart that is resistant to God.

Denial is not the only fruit, however. Some of us willingly acknowledge God's existence, but we then *distort* him into "images" that cater to our sinful hearts. This is Paul's explanation for the multiplicity of religions in the world. We took glory from the real God and assigned it to new versions of him that we preferred over him.

Furthermore, we manifest our resistance to God's glory through *disobedience*—we do what we want instead of what God wants even when we know what he wants. We'll get into that more in the next chapter.

Denial, distortion, and disobedience: three bad fruits of a heart that is resistant to God's power, glory, and authority.

So, what do you do when you realize that there's not just something wrong with the world, but something wrong with you?

Paul's answer might surprise you. The most common response, he says, is to get religious.

The problem is that religion can't really fix the problem. In fact, it just makes it worse.

~~RELIGION~~

Is Religion the Answer?

"Therefore you have no excuse, O man, every one of you who judges..." (Romans 2:1)

The twentieth-century Christian philosopher Francis Schaeffer was once asked, "If you had one hour with a modern person to talk to them about Christianity, what would you say?"

Schaeffer's reply: He'd spend the first 50 minutes trying to convince them that they are lost, because failing to see that is the reason most modern people find Christ irrelevant.

That's what Paul aims to do in the first three chapters of Romans: to make us *feel*, deep in our souls, that we're lost—that there is literally nothing we can do to repair the damage sin has caused—so that we're ready to accept the divine rescue offer. He wants us to understand that the problem is so bad that it's something only God can fix.

So, having shown us the many ways in which we suppress the truth about God, he deals with a very common response: "Well, if God's unhappy with my heart, I had better start getting religious." Paul devotes an entire two chapters of Romans to showing why this simply will not work.

I want to say this as clearly as possible: religion cannot help us. That's because, by itself, religion is powerless to reverse the curse of death that sin has released in our hearts.

I know that sounds confusing. After all, I'm a church leader. Mine is a "religious" job. I run a church, and here I am, saying that being religious is dangerous.

That's because there is a crucial difference between a religious approach to God and a gospel one—between what you might call "churchianity" and "Christianity." Religion is the gospel's number 1 competitor: the most common substitute for reconciliation with God.

Every religion in the world (except the gospel) operates according to this premise: I obey; therefore I'll be accepted. If I obey well enough and often enough, then I will earn the blessing of God (or the gods, or the universe, or whatever). The gospel turns that on its head: it says, "You are accepted; therefore obey."

Paul had grown up religious. He claimed to be the most religious Jew possible, and he had the receipts to back it up. Then he found Jesus—or rather, Jesus found him—and that made him regard all that religious activity of which he once was so proud as "dung" (Philippians 3:4-9). And now, in this part of the book of Romans, he's writing to those who grew up in religious circles like his.

The particular religion someone follows is not particularly important—what Paul says about religion in these chapters applies equally to the commandment-keeping Jew, the church-going Christian, the Koran-believing

Muslim, and even the carbon-footprint-reducing progressive. For two whole chapters Paul pleads, *Beware of religion. It cannot remedy the problem and it will only make things worse.*

Here are five things Paul says are wrong with religion.

PROBLEM #1: NO ONE MEETS THE STANDARD (OR EVEN GETS CLOSE)

In the second chapter of this letter, Paul looks right at the religious crowd and says, *Don't pretend that you live up to the standards you demand from others* (see Romans 2:1).

God's standard for what constitutes a morally good person is embodied in the Ten Commandments. Even those who don't believe in God usually acknowledge that at least some of these laws serve as good moral guidelines. So, let's do a little quiz. How naturally do keeping these come to you?

Put a check by any that you feel you always keep and an "X" by those you know you don't. And feel free to round up.

1. *You shall have no other gods before me.* Can you say, "Nothing has ever been more important to me than my relationship with God. I have never loved, trusted, or obeyed anything more than God or sought to please anything or anyone, including myself, as much as I seek to please him"? Put a check here if that's true of you... ☐

2. *You shall not make for yourself a carved image.* Can you say, "I've never imagined God according to my preferences or reshaped him according

to my prejudices. I've always fully and naturally embraced what the Bible reveals him to be"? Same deal. Check here if that's true... ☐

3. *You shall not take my name in vain.* Can you say, "I have never wielded the name of God inappropriately. I have always spoken of him with utmost reverence; nor have I been lethargic or apathetic during a time of worship. Anything that had God's name attached to it I treated with the highest degree of respect, nor have I ever damaged God's reputation by calling myself his follower while not representing him well"? ☐

4. *Remember the Sabbath day, to keep it holy.* "I've always set aside time weekly to cease from my labors and focus on, trust, and enjoy God. I've always given to God the first and best of my time and treasures. I've always lived with the freedom of knowing that my success and provision doesn't depend on me." ☐

5. *Honor your parents.* This command is really about obedience to authorities in our lives which are placed there by God—first, parents. Later that would include our teachers, the government, the police, our bosses—basically anyone that represents a legitimate authority in our lives. So, can you say, "I have always respected and obeyed authorities in my life, giving them both honor and willing obedience, whether anyone was watching or not. I have never spoken disparagingly of authority and have always submitted to it joyfully with respect and honor"? ☐

6. *You shall not kill.* Now, I know what you're thinking: "I've been waiting for this one. I should be fine here." Not so fast. Jesus explained that an attitude of hate toward someone else is, in God's eyes, just as sinful as murder (Matthew 5:21-22), which means to pass this one you have to be able to say, "Not only have I never murdered anybody; I have also never wished harm of any kind to befall someone else. I have never delighted in the misfortune or pain of someone else, even my enemies." ☐

7. *You shall not commit adultery.* Same rules as above. It's not just about the act but the thoughts that precede the act (see v27-28). Can you say, "I've never had sex with somebody outside the bonds of marriage, nor have I entertained sexual thoughts about anyone outside the bonds of marriage." I went ahead and put an "X" for you. ☒

8. *You shall not steal.* Can you say, "I've never taken anything that doesn't belong to me. That includes copying answers from a friend at school, taking credit for something I wasn't fully responsible for, or downloading illegally copied music. I've always respected the belongings, rights, and creations of others and have taken only what I have earned, and always given my employer the full amount of time I was paid for—never spending work time web-surfing, Instagramming, or tweeting"? ☐

9. *You shall not bear false witness.* "I've never bent the truth to get out of a bad situation. I've never stretched the truth to make myself look better.

I've never slandered another person. I've always fully fulfilled any promises that I've made." Again, I went ahead and put an "X" in for you. ☒

10. *You shall not covet.* Coveting means not being satisfied with what you have or intensely desiring something someone else has. Can you say, "I've never been greedy for something that was not mine, nor have I ever been jealous of the abilities, the looks, the positions, or the possessions of others. In fact, I've always rejoiced with others in what they have, even when I didn't have that thing myself and really wanted it. Furthermore, I've never complained about what God has provided for me, and I've always been thankful and fully content with what I have and where I am in life"? ☐

How did you do?

My guess is you got 0. That's what I got.

Newsflash: If you get 0 on the only exam in a course, there's no way you are passing the class.

Let's say, though, that you don't accept the Ten Commandments as the right moral code to live by. Ask yourself how well you measure up to whatever moral code you do espouse. How consistently and instinctively do you do the right thing? Francis Schaeffer asked what would happen if, when we stood before God, he revealed that each of us had walked through life with an invisible little recorder hung around our necks that only turned on whenever we said the word "ought" or "should": "He ought to... she should... they ought to... I should..." And then, on Judgment Day, God judged us by those statements alone. Would any of us, he asked, pass our own "ought" and "should" standards?

I think the answer is again, pretty clearly, "X."

So, the first problem with religion—any religion—is that all of us fail to live up to its ideals.

PROBLEM #2: MOTIVES MATTER

Actions done with wrong motives are no more pleasing to God than they are to us. If my wife found out that all my service to her—including my gifts on Christmas Day, Valentine's Day, and her birthday, and my bringing her coffee in bed every morning—all came from a guilty conscience over the fact I was really in love with someone else, would that be satisfying to her? Of course not. It's not just the action God cares about; it's the heart. Paul says that for works to be good in God's sight, they have to be done seeking God's glory and delight, not our own (Romans 2:6-7).

Growing up, my grandad used to raise pigs. He'd take slop out to feed them, and sometimes he'd let me tag along with him. The slop was the nastiest stuff you could imagine—basically just rotting food. It smelled unspeakably bad. But the pigs *loved* it. Give them the slightest opportunity and they'd devour it like it was their last meal, and the only way to keep them from the slop was to restrain them. And yet, not one time did *I* ever have to be restrained. Not once did my grandfather have to say to me, "Now, J.D., don't eat this stuff. If you do, you'll be punished." I could sit there beside it all day long, whether or not he was looking, and I'd never touch it. No rules, threats, or offers of reward were required.

God doesn't want spiritual pigs, who only stay away from the slop of sin because they are afraid of punishment. He wants sons and daughters in heaven who share his heart, who wouldn't choose sin even if they had the opportunity to.

Furthermore, good deeds done only to earn blessing or escape punishment are inherently self-seeking—the kind of good deeds Paul says God doesn't recognize as good (v 6-7). The 19th-century preacher C.H. Spurgeon illustrated this through a great story about an ancient English king and a carrot farmer. One day, the carrot farmer showed up at the king's court with the biggest carrot the king had ever seen. The farmer said, "Your Majesty, when I harvested this huge carrot, I knew it was fit for a king, so I am bringing it to you as a gift, to honor you." The king was greatly moved and said, "I own the land next to your farm, and I am going to give you 300 more acres so that you can grow more carrots and enjoy the profits."

One of the king's noblemen heard this and thought, "Wow. If the king gives 300 acres in response to a mere carrot, imagine what he'd give in response to a real gift!" So he went out that night and bought the finest horse in all of England, and the next day led it before the king. "O king," he said, "when I saw this great horse, I knew it was fit only for a king. So I am bringing it to you as a gift."

The king, being a shrewd and wise ruler, saw through the ruse. He thanked the nobleman and said nothing more. Seeing the nobleman's confused expression, he then said, "Yesterday, the carrot farmer was giving the carrot to me. Today you are giving the horse only to yourself."

A good deed done for selfish motives is not a truly good deed; the only person you are really loving through it is yourself. For deeds to be good in God's sight, they have to be done for the right reasons (God's glory) and from the right motivation (a genuine delight in the good). And if we are doing them religiously—to get back into, or keep ourselves in, God's favor—then our good deeds are really gifts to ourselves, not to him.

PROBLEM #3: RELIGION DOESN'T ADDRESS THE ROOT CAUSES OF OUR SIN

Sin's core, as Paul has explained (Romans 1:25), is a replacement of God at the center of our affections with ourselves. The essence of all the commandments, Jesus said, is "Love the Lord your God with all your heart and with all your soul and with all your mind and all your strength [and] love your neighbor as yourself" (Mark 12:30-31). If you keep all the other commandments without obeying those, it's hard to call anything in your life truly "good." And keeping religious rules does not enable anyone to love, nor does it make up for how we have all treated God.

Think of it like this: imagine you meet a guy in a hotel. He's friendly and kind, and you see him generously tip the bellhop. He's polite to everyone he meets. But then you discover that this guy is in the hotel to meet up with a woman with whom he's cheating on his wife. It would be hard for the betrayed wife to call his generosity and or good manners "good" in light of the wrong he's doing to her and their family. The larger context colors everything. It is the same with us. In the larger context of our rebellion against God, our tokens of goodness just don't seem that good.

PROBLEM #4: RELIGION CATERS TO OUR IDOLS

Religion not only fails to address our core problem, rebellion; it actually becomes a handmaid to the idols we worship in place of God. We commandeer religion to obtain the power, respect, approval, and wealth we crave. There's nothing wrong with any of those things in themselves; it's just that when we commandeer religion to obtain them, we should be honest that what we're seeking is not God but those things.

In college, I signed up for a theater class because I needed an elective from the arts department to graduate. I was more of a sports guy, and I was *not* interested in theater. But I studied diligently and did well so that I could get a good grade. After all, good grades lead to good jobs and good jobs lead to good paychecks. I studied theater not for love of theater but for love of the things that mastering theater could obtain for me. Now, 25 years later, I have a job. I have a paycheck. And guess what my wife and I enjoy doing: going to the theater. (My wife takes full credit for this transformation.) Now we spend a chunk of our hard-earned money buying theater tickets. In college, theater was a means to an end. I studied it only as a way to (eventually) get money. Now I use money to enjoy theater. What was once a means has become an end. What once was useful to me has become beautiful.

For many religious people, God is useful to them, not beautiful. When something is beautiful to you, you seek it for its own sake. When it's useful, you seek it because it is a means to something else that you really want.

To help his religious readers diagnose their hearts, Paul asks a question of his religious Jewish readers that, on the surface, sounds confusing: "You who abhor idols, do you rob temples?" (Romans 2:22). He's not accusing these uber-religious Jews of actually breaking into temples and stealing their treasures. His point is this: *The reason people go to a temple and bow down to a statue is because they think that way the statue will give them what they need—things like prosperity. If that's what brings you to the temple to worship God, you are not actually after him; you are using him to get prosperity. You are attempting to rob God—to offer him worship in hopes that you can get from him what you really want.*

Here's how you know if you're doing this: you get angry when God doesn't reward your religious obedience with some blessing. You find yourself yelling at heaven, "But God, I kept your commands. I did everything right, and I still didn't get the promotion, or the raise, or the relationship, or the children, or whatever. You've not kept up your end of the bargain." Were you obeying God for the sake of God's glory or because you thought obedience to him was the best means to something else?

PROBLEM #5: RELIGION FUELS OUR PRIDE

We tend to think that religion makes people better. At the least, it points them in the right direction. And it does. But, when pursued for self-seeking reasons, religion has the side effect of strengthening the core sickness at work in our heart: pride.

Paul identifies three manifestations of pride that religion strengthens in us:

A critical spirit: Religious people, he says, are quick to "pass judgment" (Romans 2:1). They want to show that others are worse than them because that's how they establish their goodness: by comparison. The point is not how good I am but that I'm better than you. Religious people are often quick to find fault, particularly if it's about something they are not struggling with themselves.

Hypocrisy: Religion will tend to make people hide their faults. They maintain an outward appearance of togetherness while inwardly the same passions they despise in others rage in their hearts. And often, in secret, they practice those things. Paul says, "You, who judge, practice the very same things" (v 1). How many stories do we have to hear about religious leaders who secretly engage in the very things they pontificate against from their pulpits?

Insecurity: Both of the above are driven by insecurity—insecurity over where we stand with God. Religion leaves us with the perpetually nagging question: have I done *enough*? Martin Luther, a man deeply steeped in religious rigor, admitted that this constant question of "Have I done enough?" drove him to despair and, eventually, to hating God. "I hated that word 'righteousness,'" he said, "which I had been taught to understand is the righteousness with which God punishes the unrighteous sinner."[16] In other words, he thought the righteousness of God was the standard by which he would one day be evaluated—and since that was a standard he knew he'd never meet, he secretly despised God's law even while outwardly making an impressive religious show in obeying it. This is religion at its worst.

---

16 "Preface to Latin Writings," in *Luther's Works, Volume 34, Career of the Reformer IV* (Concordia Publishing House, 1960), p 336.

Our inability to keep the laws of God drives us to despair, which drives us to judgmentalism and hypocrisy.

Religion can serve a purpose—it reveals the laws of God to us and points us in the direction we should go. In that way, it's like railroad tracks. The problem is, like a set of railroad tracks, it is powerless to move the freight along. Religion can reveal our sinfulness but can't heal it.

The gospel, as we'll see in the next chapter, is different. The gospel flips the religious premise on its head. Rather than "I obey, therefore I'm accepted," it says, "I am accepted, therefore I obey." This produces a whole different kind of obedience—an obedience motivated not by the need to be saved, but by gratefulness that we have been saved.

I love Tim Keller's summary of Paul's tirade against religion in Romans 2: "Any religion that does not begin with a deep experience of God's grace in the cross is going to leave you smug, overly sensitive, judgmental, hypocritical, and insecure." Far from curing the problem, religion, bereft of the gospel, makes us worse.

THE GOSPEL AS THE ANTI-RELIGION

Religion is all about doing. But, ironically, here is what the religious person never does: they never truly repent of who they are at their core and turn in desperation to God. "Repent" means to turn your thinking and life around—asking God to perform a "Copernican revolution" in your heart and life. What once was self-focused becomes God-focused.

As long as we are seeking to obey God well enough to earn his blessing—whether it's blessing in this life or the next one, or both—we are effectively saying, "I can do this. I can be the hero. When I arrive in heaven, I will deserve the praise for getting there."

Paul points us in the opposite direction: "God's kindness [in enabling you to experience his goodness, to hear his word, and to understand your need for mercy] is meant to lead you to repentance" (v 4). To acknowledge that we haven't lived up to his holiness, and never could. God does not call us to be religious but repentant—to return to him as the center of our lives and hopes, relying on his kindness and not on our own efforts.

So, Paul concludes his summation of the human condition in this way: "No one will be justified [declared in the right] in his sight by the works of the law, because [only] the knowledge of sin comes through the law" (Romans 3:20). To religious people he says, *Have a good look at the law you take so seriously and you'll see that, despite all your efforts, sin radiates from the core of who you are.*

All of us—religious and non-religious—"are all under sin" (v 9). That's Paul's iron-clad conclusion after three chapters.

And that means rescue can't come from within. There's nothing in there for any of us except corruption and death. We don't need to buckle down, try harder, and dig deeper. It's poisonous all the way down.

Rescue can only be found by looking up, Paul says, and that's where he turns next. But, before we turn there with him, let's hit pause for a moment and head to an intermission...

WHO IS JESUS?

At the center of Christianity is the person of Jesus. Because of that, it's impossible to have a good grasp of the Christian gospel without having a grasp of who he is. Here's our gospel definition that we introduced in chapter 1:

> *God, in an act of grace, sent his Son, Jesus, to earth as a man so that through his life, death, and resurrection he could rescue us, reign as King, and lead us into the eternal, full life we were created to enjoy.*

Before we explore how Jesus went about rescuing us, we need to pause for a minute to understand *who* Jesus actually is, because *what he did* only makes sense in light of *who he is*. Paul assumes that his readers have some knowledge of what Christians believe about Jesus, so let's stop and make sure we're all on the same page.

To get there, let's start with a Big Wheel and a bunch of unlucky ants.

HOW TO TALK WITH ANTS

My friend Joby grew up in South Carolina, and next to his house was an empty, sandy lot, pockmarked with nests full of carpenter ants. Joby loved to go there with his Big Wheel. (If you don't remember what those were, think low-slung kids' tricycle with a fat front wheel, the Harley-Davidson of tricycles. The Louis Marx Toy Company designed the Big Wheel in a way so that the rider could not see over the wheel—because road-blindness is exhilarating for every driver, particularly young children. I'm not sure how this toy ever made it past our parents.) Because the pedals attached to the front wheel, at high speed you could lock the wheel in a dead stop, and then if you turned the wheel just right you could do donuts for days. Joby loved to take his Big Wheel over to the sandy lot and skid atop the anthills, leaving in his wake billowing waves of sand and ants.

One day, some grape jelly from his sandwich dripped onto the sand, and within five minutes hundreds of ants swarmed to the spillage. So the next day, he brought over a full jar of jelly and smeared several streaks across the lot. In five minutes, each streak looked like bumper-to-bumper traffic on ant highway. At full speed he took his Big Wheel, hit the ant river, turned the wheel, and skidded across the backs of the ants like a car on an oil slick. (Note: I'm just telling the story, not advocating for it.) Every day he laid out a new jelly trap, setting up the ants for his joy-ride of death.

Say that you have a soft spot in your heart for these ants, and you are appalled by Joby's ant-ics (see what I did there?). You want to warn the ants not to take the bait of Joby's jelly. You want to tell them, "Hear me, all ye ants! Don't fall for the jelly. If you eat of this jelly, you shall surely die." If you stood above their anthills and yelled this down at them, the ants would have just looked up and said, "Oh man, look at the size of that guy's foot!" and scuttled away. The only way you could really warn the ants would be to get down on their level—to become one of them. Only then could you earn their trust, communicate with them, and lead them to safety.

But of course, that's impossible. The ants' problem is that they lack the perspective to understand the danger, and those of us with that perspective lack the ability to warn them.

It might seem strange, but let's start our discussion of Jesus' incarnation here. "Incarnation" means literally "en-flesh-ing," and it refers to that moment when Jesus, a being who had existed eternally as God, was born as a baby to Mary in a stable in Bethlehem 2,000 years ago. Jesus' mother was human, which made him fully man, but he was conceived as the Holy Spirit overshadowed her, which made him also fully God. Christians call him the God-Man, because he is both 100% God and 100% man.

At the center of Christianity is the audacious claim that the God who made this world walked in it. He came to live as one of us, in order to rescue us.

Maybe you hear the phrase "Son of God" and wonder, "Well, is he God or is he God's creation?" If he is God, does that mean there are now two Gods? And if there's only one God, who was Jesus praying to when he spoke to God? And what could Jesus possibly have meant when he said, "Not my will but yours be done," and, most significantly, "My God, my God, why have you forsaken me?" (Mark 14:36; 15:34)?

Great questions. Scripture teaches that God is a "Trinity": that is, a unity of three Persons in one Being. God exists not as a family of Gods, nor does one God put on different hats and play-act different divine roles. God exists eternally as three distinct Persons in one

Being. Christians have believed that consistently for 2,000 years.

I know, I know: the moment you try to think about it, your brain starts making a buzzing noise and wafts of smoke trail out of your ears. That's ok; I would actually find it suspicious if God's nature and character were easily grasped by tiny, finite minds. Who do we ants think we are?

To help us get our minds around the nature of God, the Bible communicates it to us, at times, through analogies. All analogies eventually break down, but these biblical ones are a helpful starting place for understanding who Jesus is.

HEBREWS: "RADIANCE" AND "IMPRINT"

The writer of the book of Hebrews describes Jesus as "the *radiance* of the glory of God and the exact *imprint* of his nature" (Hebrews 1:3, emphasis added).

"*Radiance*": The sun is so powerful that even at 93 million miles away, it still burns our skin. Decrease that distance by 1.1% to 92 million miles and we wouldn't live to complain about the sunburn. The sun is an incredible, mind-boggling, and dangerous celestial reactor. And yet, standing on earth, we delight in its warmth and enjoy its light.

Now, if you want to be technical about it, you can't actually see the sun's essence—the internal atomic reactions, the core 500 million metric tons of hydrogen fusing into helium every second. All that we see is the radiance emanating from that fusion. And yet, it would make no sense to say, "I can see the sun's radiance but not the sun itself." *To see the sun's radiance is to see the sun.* By saying that Jesus is the radiance of God, the writer of Hebrews means that Jesus is the emanation of God's nature. To see Jesus is to see God. He is the shining light of God's glorious nature. He is the glory coming off of God's face, one and the same with God.

"Imprint": The writer of Hebrews goes on to say that Jesus is the "exact imprint of God's nature." Think of it like a signet ring: for centuries, if you wanted to sign something, you'd heat wax and take your signet ring and push it down into the softened wax. What remained in the wax was the exact imprint of the ring's face. When you received an official document, you could be hundreds of miles from that ring, but you would know exactly what the shape of its face was. You understood its majesty and authority. To see one is to understand the other. The writer of Hebrews says that the natures of Jesus and the Father are the same. To see one is to see the other. Everything that God is, Jesus is.

JOHN: "WORD"

One other analogy that the Bible uses to illustrate the nature of Jesus which I find particularly helpful is "the Word." The apostle John says, "In the beginning was the Word, and the Word was with God, and the Word was God" (John 1:1).

Jesus is the Word of the Father. In one sense, our words are separate from our minds; but in another, they are inextricably linked. To hear my words is to hear me. The best I've heard this explained was in a debate between an 8th-century missionary named Timothy and one of the first Muslim caliphs. Timothy had been called in by

Muslim rulers to defend the doctrine of the Trinity, and he was trying to explain how Jesus, a man, could be God, without implying that there are two Gods.

Picking up on the apostle John's analogy of "the Word," Timothy explained that when we speak with someone, our minds think a thought: for example, "I feel hot." We then form that thought into the words of whatever language we are trying to communicate in, and then our vocal cords create vibrations in the air which carry those words to someone else's ears.

Three different things: thoughts; words; vibrations. And yet you'd never say, "I heard J.D.'s words but not J.D." My thoughts, my words, and the vibrations by which you heard those words were all part of one inseparable experience. Timothy said the Father is like the thought, the Son is the Word, and the Spirit is the wind-carried vibration that brings the thought to our ears; the Son makes the Father known to us. He is all that the Father is: the exact imprint of his nature and the radiance of his presence.

Again, it's just an analogy, but it's a helpful one.

This radiance, this word, took on flesh and dwelt among us. When we think about Jesus, we need to hold two realities together.

One: he's fully human, complete with human emotions and human limitations, just like you and me. He knows exactly what it's like to be tired, hungry, tearful, joy-filled, and distressed.

Two: he was (and is) God himself, fully divine, unlike us. He knows everything (Mark 2:1-12). He rules everything (Matthew 26:53; John 3:31-36; 17:2). He commands storms and walks on water (Matthew 8:23-27; 14:22-33). He resisted the attractions of sin and overcame sickness, disease, and death (Matthew 4:1-11, 23; 9:35; John 11:1-44). Best of all, he walked out of a grave (Matthew 28:1-10).

Because he was God, he could live the life that we, being mired in sin, were unable to live: a life of full obedience to God. But because he was human, when he lived that life and died under the penalty of sin anyway, he could release us from that curse. More on that in the next chapter.

This is the glory of Jesus: he is just like us and not like us at all. 100% man and 100% God. The God-Man. And that means that he is uniquely able to rescue us.

RESCUE

Why Do Christians Talk about "Being Saved"?

"But now the righteousness of God has been manifested apart from the law ... through faith in Jesus Christ for all who believe." (Romans 3:21-22)

The sensation of drowning is the worst feeling I've ever experienced.

My whitewater-rafting guide had told us that we were about to go through three "class 5" rapids in a row, and once we started, he said, there was no stopping. The most important thing, he said, was not to fall out in the second rapid because the second one was the most dangerous rapid on the entire river.

Obediently, I avoided falling out on the second one—by falling out on the first. The problem was that I couldn't make it back to the boat before entering the second rapid, which meant I went through the worst rapid on the Gauley River like a cork in a whirlpool. The massive torrent of water thrust me under again and again—it felt like having a gigantic waterfall crashing continually on my head. I'd pop up for a gasp of air, only to be pushed back under. Finally I felt my helmeted head smash up against something bouncy, and I opened my eyes to see one of the boats on our expedition, filled with a bunch of exchange students from China. After a few brief seconds of awkward staring, the international language of desperation kicked in, and they grabbed me and hoisted me up.

Reading Romans 1 – 3 feels to me a bit like bobbing through those rapids. Paul unloads one cascade of bad news after another. Just when your head pops up, you're shoved back under.

My heart is idolatrous. My will is rebellious. My cravings are corrupt. My religion is selfish. My motives are skewed. Even the genuinely good things I do are tainted with pride and competitiveness. God's glory, which ought to be the center of my affections, is scarcely an afterthought, even in my best moments.

A drowning person needs a rescue. These are rapids we can't swim out of.

The Christian gospel is about how God entered into the torrential forces of our sin to deliver us out of them, because he was the only one who could do that.

The "but' in Romans 3 marks one of the greatest transitions ever penned: "But now the righteousness of God has been revealed" (v 21, NIV). That's a huge "but." The righteousness of God, he explains, is not just a standard that God judges us by; it's a gift God gives to us through Christ.

What follows that "but" is what one Christian theologian

calls "the most important paragraph ever written."[17] In it, Paul uses three key words to describe God's rescue operation: justification, redemption, and propitiation. Those terms might sound unfamiliar, but they're really quite simple. And they change everything.

JUSTIFICATION

Paul says that through Christ's work on the cross, sinners can be *"justified freely* by his grace" (v 23-24).

Justified means "declared righteous." It concerns our legal status. If I am accused of a crime, there comes a point at the end of my trial when the jury foreman stands up and gives the verdict. If they announce, "Not guilty," then at that moment I am innocent, cleared, *justified*. I walk out of that courtroom a free citizen, without a stain on my character or blot on my record. Or, as my childhood pastor used to explain it, "just-as-if-I'd-never-sinned."

This is important, and it's where a lot of people go wrong: Justification does not refer to the process of actually becoming a better person. (That is important too, but in theological terms it's called sanctification.) Justification has to do with your legal status before God. Martin Luther said that the justified Christian was "simultaneously righteous and a sinner." God declares us to be righteous before we are, in actuality, righteous in our behavior. Our righteousness, in God's eyes, is now based on the righteousness of Christ which has been credited to our account.

---

17 Leon Morris, *The Epistle to the Romans* (Eerdmans, 1988), p 173.

This transfer of righteousness was pictured in the sacrifices that God had Jews offer to him in the centuries preceding Jesus' birth. Each believing family would bring a lamb—a perfect, unblemished lamb—and they would lay it on the altar and place their hand on its head, confessing their sin. The lamb's throat was cut. In that moment, they were justified because the lamb was punished for their sin. The lamb died there on the altar, and they walked home free.

This was a foreshadowing of what Jesus would do and how believers would receive him. On the cross Jesus became our sin, so that when I lay my hand of faith on him—when I trust in him as the one who has saved me, personally—my sin becomes his and his righteousness becomes mine. On the cross Jesus became the liar, the thief, the adulterer, and the murderer. He became the husband who has neglected or abused his family. He became the immoral woman who wrecked someone else's marriage. He became the drug addict. The teenage girl lying to her parents. The hypocrite living a double life. He became the proud, the selfish, and the apathetic. He became those things and died for them so that you and I, by trusting in him, could become innocent of them: Justified.

REDEMPTION

> "... *through the redemption that is in Christ Jesus.*"
> *(Romans 3:24)*

Redemption means "to buy something back." Imagine you are short of cash and so you take your vintage collection of signed Nicolas Cage posters to a pawn shop. Sad day. A little while later, you inherit a modest fortune from an uncle, and so you head back to the pawn shop. Surprisingly, no one has bought the posters. So you fork out the ransom price to buy those masterpieces back. What have you just done? You've redeemed Nicolas Cage. You have brought him back home to the center of your mantle, where he belongs.

Or, you can "redeem" a coupon. You're in line at the grocery store, buying some Doritos and M&Ms, and when the receipt prints out, it says, "Congratulations— you've been chosen to receive a free ham. Just present this coupon at checkout." So, you go back and get the ham, and you bring it back to the checkout line, and the cashier says, "That'll be $23." And you think, "Well, maybe for your average shopper it's $23, but not for me. I have a coupon." You hand the coupon to her, and the ham is redeemed. Free ham. What did you pay? Nothing. What did the manufacturer pay? Full price. The pig, of course, is the real hero because the pig paid it all. Your coupon just availed you of everyone's generosity.

Right before he died, Jesus shouted a single word: "*Tetelestai*," which we translate as "It is finished" (John 19:30). It's actually an ancient banking term, meaning "It is paid." Archaeologists have found 1st-century receipts marking the moment when someone paid off a debt, and across the receipt is scrawled the word *Tetelestai*—it's been paid. That's what Jesus was saying as he died—*It's been paid. I've paid the price to buy you back from death, for life—from sin, for God.* There's nothing left for you to pay, nothing left for you to do, in order to be right with God. Jesus offers redemption. It costs you nothing because it cost him everything.

PROPITIATION

> "... *Christ Jesus, whom God put forward as a propitiation by his blood.*" *(Romans 3:25)*

This might be the word we're least familiar with. It means that God's wrath has been satisfied; his claim against us is settled. When a debt has been fully paid, the collector has no more claim on the borrower. God no longer has a claim on someone who trusts Jesus, because in Jesus God took all his righteous anger against their sin into himself. On the cross, the judgment that we deserved was placed on him.

Some find it difficult to think of, or worship, a God who could be angry at us. After all, the Bible itself tells us that "God is love," right? But God's anger toward sinners is not in contradiction with his love for sinners—in fact, his anger flows out of his love. *Because* God loves his glory and his creation, he is angry at the sin that destroys it. Glory and justice are the foundation of his throne, the ultimate source of beauty in everything that's ever been beautiful. And he loves his image-bearers, us, and grieves over what sin has done to us. After all, when you love somebody, you can't help but hate the things that destroy them. If you love someone, you hate the cancer eating away at their body or the addiction destroying their lives. That is how God feels about our sin. God hates it, and he is rightfully angry at it. He couldn't be a just and loving God and not feel that way.

So he provided a way to separate us from our sin. He took the wrath, corruption and ultimate consequences of sin into himself, and offered that deliverance to all who would receive it.

Maybe you ask, "Why couldn't God have just wiped the slate clean, healed us, and started over? Why require a sacrifice to forgive?"

Good question, and it has to do with the nature of forgiveness. True forgiveness, you see, is always costly and requires suffering on the part of the forgiver. Imagine you steal my car and you wreck it. And you come to me and say, "J.D., I'm sorry. I stole your car, and I wrecked it. And I don't have the money to pay for the repair." What are my options? Option one: I take you to court, sue you, and make you pay back the damage in full. Option two: I can say, "I forgive you. No need to pay." Who then pays the cost of repairs? I do.

Or say, for example, you lied about me, causing me irreparable reputational damage. Months later, you come and ask for forgiveness. What are my choices? I can vent my anger on you. I could go out and tell everyone what you did, forever ruining your chances of doing business with them. Both are understandable options. But if I choose to forgive you, I agree to let the sting of your sin die inside of me. You will receive no judgment for your sin; you will not have to go through the same pain you caused me. This is what God did at the cross.

If God simply ignored the injustice of sin, that would itself be unjust. The Old Testament book of Proverbs says, "Acquitting the guilty and condemning the innocent: the LORD hates both of those things" (17:15). God's just moral order, which is the foundation of his throne (Psalm 89:14), had to be restored; the debt against justice had to be paid. Righteous anger must be directed somewhere. So God chose to absorb the penalty, anger, and shame of sin into himself. On the cross, the Son of God shielded us from God's righteous wrath by taking it in our place. In him, God's wrath was propitiated, we were justified, and our broken lives were redeemed.

And thus, through the cross, Paul says, God was able to accomplish two things that seemed like they were hopelessly at odds: he satisfied the full demands of his justice—upholding his glory which upholds the universe—*and* he saved us. At the cross, he became...

> *"... just **and** the justifier of the one who has faith in Jesus." (Romans 3:26, emphasis added)*

The cross was not just Jesus *demonstrating* God's love for us, as if through it was merely saying, "Here's how much I love you!" and then dying a dramatic death to prove the depth of his love. No, at the cross, God was literally taking our place in punishment. Jesus didn't just die for us; he died instead of us.

Some like to imagine Jesus' death as merely a great demonstration of sacrifice, kind of like a martyr's kiss, proving once and for all his great love. But if Jesus' death was not accomplishing something for sinners, how was it love? Imagine I am walking along the side of a busy road with my kids and I say to them, "Do you know how much daddy loves you? Watch this!" and I jump in front of a ten-ton truck roaring down the highway. That's not love. That's idiocy. The only way it is love is if my jumping in front of the truck somehow saved them—if by doing so, I pushed them out of the truck's way.

That is what Jesus did for sinners like us on the cross. The cross is the measure of his love. There is no distance he will not go to hold out forgiveness to you. He even went through hell for you, instead of you. That is love.

JESUS IN MY PLACE

So, there you have it. Three words that describe God's rescue plan—*justification, redemption, propitiation.*

If you're looking for an even easier way to remember it, here are four (much shorter) words:

Jesus in my place.

Jesus lived the life I should have lived—a life without sin—and then died the death I should have died— under the condemnation of sin. He took my place—he received the punishment I deserved, so I could receive the acceptance he deserved. Paul uses lots of words to describe the dazzling diamond of salvation, but the core of it is this: Jesus lived a life I should have lived and then died the death I was condemned to die, so that I could be made right with God forever.

THE GREATEST MARRIAGE OF ALL TIME

On July 28th 2000, I stood in front of a crowd of family and friends and pledged the rest of my life to a beautiful girl named Veronica McPeters. We had dated for 18 months, and on that Saturday in July our lives became one. My assets became hers, and hers became mine. No question, I got the better end of that deal, but one thing that did work in her favor was that she got my car. Because I already had a job, I had a really, really nice car and some money saved up. She had just graduated, so she had no job, a significant amount of school debt, and a tiny beater car with no air conditioning that looked like it might fall apart if it went over a speed bump too quickly. After we got married, I thought, "I can't have her drive that car," so I took hers, and she got mine. Then we used my savings account to pay off her school debt. All that was mine was hers, and all that was hers was mine.

That was July 28th 2000. On March 30th, 1989, something similar had happened with me and Jesus. I joined myself to him. He took all that was mine: my sin, my shame, and my judgment. And I got all that was his: his righteousness, his position, his reward, and his future.

Everything shameful I've ever done has been taken by Jesus on the cross, and in its place I have received Jesus' righteousness. In Romans 8, Paul exults, "There is now no condemnation for those who are in Christ" (8:1). He took it all.

Not only that, but all that belonged to Jesus has become mine! I have his favored spot at the table, his promises, his inheritance, his future. I am as sure of heaven as he is—not because I believe my life is so righteous that I've earned my place, but because Jesus gave me his place.

More than just giving me security in death, this also gives me confidence in life. Not only do I not have to fear God's judgment later; I don't have to live in fear of others' judgment now. Jesus has already seen my messed-up heart, and he has embraced me, forgiven me, and promised to change me. In the eyes of the only one whose opinion really matters, I am spotlessly righteous. That makes what others think about me less important. I love how counselor Paul Tripp says it:

> "I'm not afraid of others seeing my weakness, because nothing can ever be uncovered about me that God has not already seen and covered by the blood of Jesus." [18]

---

18 Talk given at The Summit Church in Raleigh, NC, February, 2020.

Because of the cross, I know I have peace with God. I know he is working in me, through me, and around me in all things for my good, just as he promised (Romans 8:28-29). And I know that since he's the God who died for me when I was his enemy, he'll surely take care of me now that I'm his son (Romans 5:10).

I'm justified, redeemed, forgiven, saved, rescued, and restored. And it's all by grace—all because of his undeserved kindness. This rescue, started by grace, is sustained by grace, and it will finish by grace. Whatever today brings, I know God is for me, with me, before me and behind me. Whatever tomorrow threatens, I know he's already there, making a way for me in it and through it. That is the source of a unique, deep, unassailable confidence.

NOT ASKING FOR OUR HELP

This is why Christians talk about the need to be saved. Honestly, over the years I've tried to find a different word to encapsulate the experience of meeting Jesus, because the word "saved" (at least in the part of the world I am from) sounds fundamentalist. It conjures up the image of a country preacher in a too-small suit aspirating the word in three syllables at the top of his hoarse voice as his eyes bulge out of his head. I would love something that sounds more sophisticated, more elegant. But does any other word do justice to what Jesus has actually done for us? He didn't assist us, correct us, educate us, reform us, enhance us, or inspire us—he *saved* us.

We started this chapter thinking about drowning. Let's end equally upbeat, by thinking about a car wreck.

Imagine you awaken to find yourself on a stretcher in the back of an ambulance. You're not quite sure how you got there, but as you feel panic rising in your heart, the EMT (emergency medical technician) puts their hand calmly on your head and says, "You were in a really serious wreck, and you lost a lot of blood. But thankfully we got to you in time. We've stabilized you, and we're taking you to the hospital, where you'll make a full recovery. You're going to be ok." At that point, the EMT is not asking you to do anything. You just need to trust them to keep their promise.

This is what happens to us in salvation. Sin wrecked our relationship with God and destroyed our future. Discovering the gospel is like waking up on a stretcher looking at Jesus, who says, *I've got this. I saved you. I can restore you. You're going to be ok, now and for eternity.* All you have to do—all you can do—is trust him and let him work, going along with whatever he tells you to do.

Trusting God to keep his promise is called the life of faith, and it's where the apostle Paul turns next.

FAITH

Can Anyone Actually *Know* They'll Go to Heaven?

"And to the one who does not work but believes in him who justifies the ungodly, his faith is counted as righteousness..." (Romans 4:5)

If there were a Guinness World Record for the amount of times someone asked Jesus to save them, I'm pretty sure I'd hold it.

By the time I was 19, I'd "become a Christian" about 5,000 times. Every time my church gave an invitation to pray a prayer to "accept Jesus," I did so, right then. One year my church had a goal of 300 conversions. I think I fulfilled that goal all by myself.

I know that sounds neurotic, but I just wanted to be sure that I was saved. I was plagued with questions like "Last time I prayed that, did I feel sorry enough about my sins?" and "Since praying the prayer, have I followed Jesus closely enough?"

I knew the Bible said that we were "saved [by] faith," (Ephesians 2:8) but I wanted to know: what was the faith that saves, and how could I be sure I had it?

I've since found that a lot of Christians have these same questions. Ask 20 different people what "faith" is, and you'll likely get as many different answers. Some think of it as a general sense that God is real. Others think it means sincerity in religion. They say, "I'm getting more serious about my faith." Some think having faith just means adopting a positive, hopeful outlook on life. Others think it just means that at some point you prayed the infamous "sinner's prayer," asking Jesus into your heart.

So here's the question we want to consider in this chapter: what, according to Paul, is the faith that saves, and how can we know that we have it?

So glad you asked, says Paul. After describing the components of the Great Rescue, in Romans 4 Paul offers us an analysis of what the faith that saves really is and how we can know if we have it. He takes faith and lays it out on the table, so to speak, and dissects it for you. He does that by looking at the faith of one of the most important figures in the Bible, Abraham, who lived nearly 1,800 years before Jesus was born and was the biological ancestor of the nation of Israel, regarded by both Jews and Christians alike as the "father of faith." Surely, Paul reasons, if he's the father of faith, we can learn what the faith that saves is by looking at him.

BELIEVING A PROMISE

Paul starts Abraham's story by reaching back to Genesis 15, where the writer of Genesis says, "Abraham believed God, and it was credited to him for righteousness" (Romans 4:3, CSB, quoting Genesis 15:6).

Let's go back in time to that story. In Genesis 12, God gave Abraham some pretty staggering promises—a huge family, a land to live in, eternal friendship with God, and a plan to use his family to bring healing to the world.

There was just one problem: Abraham and his wife, Sarah, were old—as in "one foot in the grave and one foot on a banana peel" old—but still childless. For nearly 50 years they had unsuccessfully tried to have kids, and now God was telling a nearly-80-year-old Abraham that he would be the father of a great nation. Sure, Rome is not built in a day, but Abraham didn't even have the first brick! And when you and your wife are octogenarians, you've pretty much pulled the curtain on that part of your life. At that point, not even the blue pill offers a lot of hope.

A few years after God first made that promise to Abraham, Genesis 15 recounts a conversation between God and Abraham (who at that point was called Abram—God added the "ha" later on). God reiterated his promise:

> "Don't worry, Abram; I am going to make you the father of a great nation, and that great nation will one day bless people all over the world by restoring them to a relationship with me."

> "Ok, God, but without wanting to get too bogged down in the details... I'm childless."

> "You're going to have a son. In fact, look at the stars. That's how big your family's going to be. Just wait."

Abram's response? "Abram believed God, and it was credited to him for righteousness." In Romans, Paul quotes that verse and says that this is a demonstration of the faith that saves. God made a huge promise; Abraham believed it and then rearranged his life around it. He and Sarah built themselves a nursery, started picking out baby names, and commenced a search for a homeland to house the new nation.

That faith, Paul said, was "credited" to Abraham as righteousness. "Credited" is a banking term (in Greek, it's *logizomai*). It means an amount gets posted to your account. For example, my son has a bank account with $106 in it. If I found out I only had a week to live and wanted to transfer all my assets to him, I would go to the bank and say, "I want you to take my entire savings account and *credit* it to my son's account." All my son would need to do to receive that money is, well, receive it. He'd just need to say "Yes."

Faith is saying yes to God's offer. That was what Abraham did. And it was his *trust in God* that God counted as righteousness. God did not justify Abraham because Abraham acted flawlessly from that point forward, but because Abraham trusted God to keep his promise.

None of us today have received a direct promise from God that we're going to have kids in our nineties (which will be a relief to most of us). But Paul says we have, in essence, been given the same promise as Abraham— the promise of eternal life with God—and so he says, "The words 'it was credited to him' were written not for [Abraham] alone, but also for us" (Romans 4:23-24, NIV). Christians trust God to keep his promise to them just as Abraham trusted God to keep his promise to him. If we believe that God has forgiven our sins in Jesus, just as he promised (v 25), then, like Abraham, our faith is credited to us as righteousness. That's the faith that saves.

As Martin Luther said, "The law says, 'Do this,' and it is never done. Grace says, 'Believe in this,' and everything is already done."[19]

FAITH'S POSTURE

Abraham's life, then, shows us that the faith that saves is believing God's promise and resting on it. The only difference between our faith and Abraham's is that Abraham looked *forward*, believing God's promise to *send* salvation; you and I look *backward*, believing he *has* sent it.

I often compare saving faith to sitting down in a chair. Perhaps you are seated now. If so, that means that there was a moment in which you looked at the chair, assessed that it was strong enough to hold you, and transferred the weight of your body from your feet to the chair. You may not even remember that moment, but your mind did a quick, subconscious assessment and you committed your weight to it. It would have been embarrassing (and painful) if the chair had failed you. But, full of confidence in the chair's manufacturers, you sat down.

Saving faith in Christ is believing that he is able to save you, just as he promised, and transferring your hope of salvation from your own goodness to his grace. It means turning over complete control of your life to him, no longer trusting yourself to guide you through life but instead surrendering to him. Right now you are either "standing," that is, relying on yourself, or you have "sat down" in surrender to Jesus. It's one or the other.

---

19 Thesis 26.

FAITH'S BOAST

Abraham's life shows us a second important thing about faith—where faith places its confidence.

> "[Abraham] did not waver in unbelief at God's promise
> but was strengthened in his faith and gave glory to
> God, because he was fully convinced that what God had
> promised, he was also able to do." (Romans 4:20-21)

Because Abraham leaned fully on God to provide him with a son, when it happened, he directed all the glory to God. If Abraham had had kids in his own strength when he was 90, he would have said, *Look at me! I'm MegaMan!* But as it stands now, Abraham will not be strutting around heaven bragging about what a rare male specimen he was. Instead he'll say, *I was a miserable, dried-up failure. Sarah and I had no hope for a son. God did it all.*

If any of our salvation came from our own strength, when we got to heaven, we'd boast about our own moral strength: "I dug deep and tried hard and said no to temptation and obeyed God and here I am." But no one will say that in heaven. As a famous hymn, "Amazing Grace," puts it, "When we've been there ten thousand years, bright shining as the sun, we've no less days to sing God's praise than when we first begun!" In heaven, God's grace will be our boast, because that's the only way any of us will be there. He, and he alone, will get the glory. Faith puts its confidence in God.

FAITH DOESN'T EXCLUDE EFFORT, BUT IT DOES EXCLUDE EARNING

To possess saving faith does not mean that we stop seeking to obey God or that we treat his commands as optional. A lot of people in church talk as if saving faith is a prayer you pray, like a rite of passage or sacred ritual that you go through once and then you're done. Because we are saved by grace (undeserved kindness), they say, whether or not we actually follow Jesus is irrelevant.

But notice how Paul talks about Abraham's faith— Abraham's faith was a choice he made to start following God which he maintained for the rest of his life. That first choice to trust God was *ratified* by a lifetime of ensuing ones.

To bring it back to our analogy of the chair, faith does not take a quick seat in the chair and pop back up. Faith takes a seat in the chair and remains in that posture for the rest of life. All of us Christians have moments when we struggle and we find ourselves back on our feet again, taking matters back into our own hands, doing our thing our way. But if we're truly saved, eventually we come back to that posture of "sitting."

Faith does not exclude effort. What it excludes is *earning*. In what I think might be one of the most important verses about salvation in the whole Bible, Paul says:

> "*Now to the one who works, pay is not credited as a gift,*
> *but as something owed.*" *(v 4)*

The premise of every job you've ever worked is this: do the work and get paid. When you are finished with your shift and the boss pays you, they are not giving you a gift, but what you are owed.

Most people approach God with the same premise: I do good things, and God pays me with heaven. "I obey, and therefore I will be accepted." Acceptance is the reward for obedience.

The gospel works from a different premise. Acceptance is given as a gift, not a reward. Paul continues:

> *"But to the one who does not work, but believes on him who declares the ungodly to be righteous, his faith is credited for righteousness." (Romans 4:5, NIV)*

By "does not work," Paul means that you stop trying to earn God's acceptance by your good work and, instead, you believe God when he says that Christ paid for the sins of the ungodly and made them righteous (5:6-9). That is, you believe God's promise that he is gracious enough to give it to you as a gift purchased by Christ. When you believe that, and accept it as your own, Christ's righteousness is credited (*logizomai*, accounted) to you. You continue to do good works—not in order to be accepted by God, but because you love the God who has accepted you.

FAITH IS ALL IN

You might be thinking, "This all sounds pretty simple." And it is. Transfer trust from yourself to God and what he has done in the death and resurrection of Jesus, and you're saved. You're justified. You possess eternal life. Romans 10:9-10 says,

> *"If you confess with your mouth that Jesus is Lord and believe in your heart that God raised him from the dead, you will be saved. For with the heart one believes and is justified, and with the mouth one confesses and is saved."*

The concept may simple, but living out this kind of trust is hard. Transferring the weight of your life from your own two feet to Jesus, and Jesus alone, can be scary.

God called Abraham to let everything go, leaving all that he had owned and called his own, and set out for a land God would show him (Genesis 12:1). If God didn't keep his promise, Abraham would have... nothing. Which is why most of us prefer a type of "faith" allows us to hedge our bets.

A lot of people prefer what I like to call a "mutual-fund faith," where we mitigate the risks of leaving all to follow Jesus.[20] In the financial world, a mutual fund is a way of spreading out your investment risk. Instead of putting all your money into one company, a mutual fund spreads your money over hundreds of companies so that if one fails, you can make it up with the others.

That's fine as an investment strategy, but it won't work as a faith strategy. The faith that saves is the faith that puts *all* its hope in God and leans *all* its weight on his promise.

So, that's the question: Have you gone *all in*?

Many of us would struggle to answer yes without qualification. We may have gone some of the way with Jesus, but we hang on to a few things, just in case things don't work out as planned. We want to keep a safety net; to hedge our bets. What might that look like? It might mean...

- presenting one way at church and another at work, school, or book club.

- getting religious but not becoming a full-on Jesus follower.

---

20 I first heard this phrase from Pastor Tony Evans: "Without a Doubt: The Assurance of Salvation (Part 3), Assurance and Faith," sermon on Romans 4:1-5, preached on July 12, 1998.

- putting limits on what you'll believe or what you'll do.

- living a morally upright life but not one that takes Jesus' call to mission seriously.

- prioritizing career advancement, sports, leisure time, and family time over involvement in God's kingdom.

"Hedging your bets" means pulling back from full obedience in any area because you are not convinced God's way is the best way, or you are afraid that God may not fully provide what you need.

Saving faith goes all in.

FAITH LOOKS UP WHEN WE FALL DOWN

At this point, you might be feeling overwhelmed. Who lives with consistent, unbroken faith? How can you ever achieve the faith of a spiritual giant like Abraham?

Well, it's interesting that you bring that up. Abraham didn't live a flawless life of faith, either, which leads to my favorite insight from Paul about Abraham's faith:

Faith looks up when we fall down.

Faith means believing that God will keep his promise even when we've broken ours. As Paul gives his whistle-stop biography of Abraham, he says that Abraham "did not waver in unbelief" (Romans 4:20, CSB). That's an odd summary of Abraham's life, considering that shortly after God had first made his promises to Abraham, Abraham did, in fact, fall flat on his face. Abraham got scared, and instead of trusting God to provide, he retreated to Egypt.

There, Pharaoh showed some interest in his wife, and instead of trusting God, Abraham told Pharaoh that Sarah was his sister so that Pharaoh wouldn't kill him and steal her. God had to rescue Sarah himself because Abraham was too cowardly to stand up for her (Genesis 12:10-20).

Then, get this: years later, *Abraham did the exact same thing, again,* with a different king. Poor Sarah! God had to rescue Sarah from Abraham's cowardice a second time (Genesis 20:1-18)! And then there's the episode in which Abraham lost confidence that God would fulfill his promise to provide a son, so he impregnated a servant girl to "help" God out. This was clearly a hedged bet (and a horrifically unjust one, to boot).

Paul knew all this and still said that Abraham "did not waver" in unbelief. How could he say that? It's because he understood that "not wavering" has less to do with never falling than it does with where you look when you fall.

Go back and read that sentence again.

Abraham fell, but he got up again with confidence that his failings did not negate God's promise. A verse in Proverbs sums this up:

> *"The righteous falls seven times and rises again."*
> *(Proverbs 24:16)*

Imagine walking along in a store behind a man who fell *seven times.* The first time you'd offer to help him up. Maybe you'd offer again the second and third also. By the fourth time, you're calling an ambulance. A person who falls seven times in a row needs to be in a hospital.

The righteous person, Proverbs says, falls continually. So much so that you wonder if they are safe out on the street. But—and this is key—*they always get back up looking at God.* The righteous person doesn't show their righteousness by never falling but by where they look *when* they fall.

I can imagine Abraham saying to God, *Oh boy, I know I have messed up again. But thank you that your promise is still true. Thank you that it's not conditional on me not falling. Thank you that it depends on you, not on me. My faith is feeble, God, but you are not, and so the promise is secure.*

This is the faith that is credited as righteousness. I fall all the time, but I believe God will keep his promise—despite me, not because of me. The Christian life is begun, sustained, and completed by faith—faith not in your ability to complete the journey but in his promise to complete it for and through you.

YOUR TURN TO ANSWER

Preachers often ask people this question: "If you died tonight and God were to say, 'Why should I let you into heaven?' what would you say?" (We never seem to consider that people might die during the day.) The question has become a cliché, but it's actually a good one to consider. What *would* you say?

Many say, "Because I was a good person." "Because I tried my best." "Because I was a sincere Christian and always tried to live out what I believed."

The faith that *saves* always starts its answer with "Because Jesus..." It would never start with "Because I..." Why? Because any answer that starts with me is going to reveal faith in my work, not faith in his. The faith that saves is the faith that leans all its hope for heaven, and for life, on Jesus Christ.

How you answer that question, then, is how you can know whether you have the faith that saves. This is how the younger, sinner's-prayer-praying, baptism-junkie J.D. could have stopped worrying about whether he'd prayed some prayer well enough or felt sorry deeply enough or gotten committed to Jesus strongly enough to be saved. I could have rested in the fact that he did what he said he did. This is how you can live with a confidence undiminished by unchosen circumstances or unsuccessful Christian living, free of anxiety about how this life will go and what will happen to you in the next one.

Why should God let you into heaven?

"Because Jesus died and rose to take my sins and give me his righteousness."

This is my answer. It echoes Abraham's.

What's yours?

FAITH IS A CHOICE

Let me close this chapter by reminding you that all that Jesus did for sinners, and all that he offers you, will be yours only if you receive it. His sacrifice does you no good if you never accept it as your own.

I recently read what must be the most bizarre Supreme Court case of all time—United States v. Wilson (1833). The defendant, George Wilson, pleaded guilty to several counts of robbery and "endangering the life of a mail driver." This was apparently a serious enough combination of crimes in 1833 to warrant execution, and Wilson was sentenced to die by hanging. President Andrew Jackson, however, for reasons unknown to us, issued Wilson with a full pardon. But then Wilson (also for reasons unknown to us) refused the pardon and demanded to pay for his crimes. The warden told Wilson he couldn't execute him; he'd been pardoned. Wilson refused the pardon. The odd case went all the way to the Supreme Court, and this was their verdict:

> *"A pardon is an act of grace ... which exempts the individual on whom it is bestowed from the punishment the law inflicts for a crime he has committed ... A pardon is a deed, to the validity of which delivery is essential, and delivery is not complete without acceptance. It may then be rejected ... and if it be rejected, we have discovered no power in a court to force it on him."* [21]

A pardon is only valid if it's accepted. God's offer is similar. He has extended the pardon to you, but you are free, like George Wilson was, to reject it.

But why would you?

---

21 https://openjurist.org/32/us/150/united-states-v-george-wilson (accessed July 7, 2022).

BUT IS IT TRUE?

Let's hit pause again. At this point in the book, maybe you're saying something like this:

*This all sounds amazing—having God as my Father, the assurance that my sins are forgiven, and the promise that I will be resurrected to eternal bliss forever. This sounds wonderful! But so do stories about Iron Man, Wakanda, Neverland, and Santa Claus. The problem with fairy tales is not that they're not great stories but that they're not true. So, yes, maybe the whole Jesus story is good—but how can we know that this stuff **actually** happened and that it's not just wishful thinking?*

Great questions. Let's rewind back to Paul's opening words in Romans, where he explains to us why he not only believes the Christian gospel, but has staked his life on it.

The first time Paul mentions the word "gospel" in Romans, he says it is about Jesus, who "was declared to be the Son of God in power ... by his resurrection from the dead" (Romans 1:1, 3-4).

Paul points to an event, the resurrection, that he claims occurred in actual history, according to specific prophecies and in the presence of a number of eyewitnesses (see 1 Corinthians 15:1-9). He, the other apostles, and the earliest Christians staked their lives on the claim that it actually happened.

In one of his other letters, Paul tells a group of Christians in the city of Corinth that if Jesus rose from the dead, it's all true, and if he didn't, this is a hoax and you are free to seek your spiritual "fix" somewhere else (1 Corinthians 15:19). So, the crucial question is, did Jesus actually rise from the dead?

Paul doesn't spend much time in Romans arguing for the fact of the resurrection, but here's how he puts it in his first letter to the Corinthians, written a few years before Romans:

> "For I delivered to you as of first importance what I also received: that Christ died for our sins in accordance with the Scriptures, that he was buried, that he was raised on the third day in accordance with the Scriptures, and that he appeared to Cephas, then to the twelve. Then he appeared to more than five hundred brothers at one time, most of whom are still alive, though some have fallen asleep. Then he appeared to James, then to all the apostles. Last of all, as to one untimely born, he appeared also to me."
>
> (1 Corinthians 15:3-8)

Paul points to two pieces of evidence crucial to early Christian testimony to substantiate his claim—the empty tomb and a significant number of eyewitnesses, most of whom were still alive at the time of Paul's writings.

Oxford scholar N.T. Wright notes that these facts *together*—the empty tomb and the eyewitnesses—are crucial parts of the case for the resurrection. If we only had an empty tomb but no eyewitnesses, skeptics would have concluded that the body was stolen. If there were only eyewitnesses but no empty tomb, skeptics would have concluded that the witnesses were deluded. The two together, however, make for convincing evidence.

More recently, some critics have speculated that the *earliest* believers didn't actually believe in Jesus' physical resurrection—that "the resurrection" was a legend that grew up over time as early Christians felt the need to "beef up" their authority. A good miracle, after all, helps anybody's credibility. The message, they speculate, began with "Jesus lives on in our hearts," but little by little it morphed into "Jesus physically rose from the dead, left an empty tomb, and appeared to eyewitnesses."

The trouble with this line of thinking is simple: Paul's letter to the Corinthians (quoted above) was written in AD 53, only 20 years after Jesus' death. (Note: not even secular scholars dispute that date for Paul's letter to the Corinthians or Paul's authorship of it.) And in this extremely early letter, Paul not only indicates there is a widespread belief in the physical resurrection of Jesus; he actually *quotes* a hymn commonly sung in the early church about the resurrection. That means belief in the resurrection was so common they'd come up with songs about it that they sang in churches. Even the uber-skeptical scholar Gerd Lüdemann says that the writing of this hymn quoted by Paul in 1 Corinthians 15:3 likely dates to within *two years* of the crucifixion.

What's the significance of that? Well, that's simply too early for a legend to grow up. Too many people were still alive who had been present during the actual events for a fantasy story to emerge uncontested.

Think of it like this: you may remember when NASCAR great Dale Earnhardt Sr. died in the final turn of the Daytona 500. That was in 2001. Maybe you watched it as it happened. Maybe me bringing it up makes you want to pause for a moment of silence. But just imagine if a friend started telling everyone they knew, "Dale actually resurrected that day. Yup, right on the track. He stepped out of the car, ran around the track a few times, pumped his fist to the crowd, held up the immortal #3, and then the #3 car lifted miraculously up off the ground and flew straight up to glory."

Even if we didn't have the video footage available to refute that, you might say, "That's not true. I stayed glued to the TV for three hours that day, watching the story unfold, and that never happened." Or, you might say, "I know a guy who knows a guy who was there. He says no such thing occurred. Ask any of the 150,000 people who were there. They all say that's not true." You might find a few gullible loons willing to go along with the "flying #3 theory." But the vast majority would say, "That's not what happened."

In 1 Corinthians 15 Paul essentially says, *Guys, if you doubt what I'm saying, go ask the people who were there. There were lots of them. They are still around. They saw him. A bunch of us saw him together.*

I point this out because it's become popular among skeptics to say that Christianity's miraculous claims emerged imperceptibly, as one generation repeated the stories about Jesus to the next, the story growing slightly each time it was retold. The New Testament skeptic Bart Ehrman says the myth of the resurrection developed in the same way that facts gets distorted in the "telephone game" which you may have played at a party.[22] It's the game where everyone sits in a circle and one person whispers some secret set of facts to another, and then that person repeats it to the person next to them, and then that person attempts to whisper those same facts to the person next to them, and on and on until the whispers make it all the way back to the original person. The big reveal is always humorous. Something that started out like "I asked the pretty girl by the punch bowl if she would like to dance," transmogrifies into "I told the girl at the bowling alley that she looked fat in those pants, and she punched me."

In essence, Ehrman says, generations of Christians did the same thing with the stories of Jesus: each repetition shifted the narrative a little in the direction of the supernatural, until what was written down years later was fundamentally different from what the apostles had first said.

But the dating of 1 Corinthians alone demonstrates that the time gap is not sufficient for that kind of message corruption! All the original apostles and eyewitnesses to the resurrection, Paul said, were still around to verify his version of it! To stay with the telephone-game analogy, it would be as if no one whispered, and the original secret-teller could hear what one person was saying to the next and was allowed to correct each deviation in real time. By the time the set of facts got back to them, it would be the same as the original transmission.

The point to take away from all of this is that Paul's letters to the Romans and the Corinthians demonstrate, beyond

---

22 *The New Testament: A Historical Introduction to the Early Christian Writings,* 5th edition (Oxford University Press, 2012), p 72-74.

reasonable doubt, that belief in a physical resurrection was part of the early church's testimony from the beginning. Which means if it's not true, they had to be hallucinating or lying.

Perhaps the skeptic says, "Maybe this group of pre-modern people experienced some kind of group hysteria that grew out of wishful thinking." Paul's answer: *Five hundred people don't typically hallucinate at once, hearing and seeing the same things and all corroborating the same story.*

"But maybe," our skeptical friend objects, "these apparent witnesses were so preconditioned to believe in the resurrection that they were gullible and superstitious, ready to accept the flimsiest of 'evidence.'" The problem with that is that religious Jews in the 1st-century were *not* preconditioned to believe in a resurrection. N.T. Wright amply demonstrates that 1st-century Jews had *no* category for a rescuer-king, a "Messiah," who would die and rise again. They were looking for a Messiah, but not a humiliated, executed one. What Jesus did went against all their expectations, to the point that even those who wanted to believe in him found it difficult to do so (see the story of Thomas, John 20:24-29). Jesus' resurrection did not fulfill their expectations but overturned them. The apostle Paul, himself an ardently religious Jew, had built his whole life around Jesus being an impostor. God's Messiah could not have shamefully died at the hands of the Romans. It was only when he was confronted with irrefutable evidence of the resurrection that he changed his mind (1 Corinthians 15:8; see Acts 9:1-9).

"Well," the skeptic continues, "maybe those 'witnesses' were just flat-out lying. After all, lots of people live for lies—many even die for them. The earliest Christians needed the 'miracle' stuff to get people to believe them. It was a 'the ends justify the means' thing in their minds."

The problem with that theory is this: what would motivate them to propagate that lie? Sure, lots of people die for a lie, but when you propagate something you *know* is a lie, you're seeking to gain something—money, safety, political power, prestige, sex, and so on. But the apostles' claim—that they had seen the risen Jesus and he was Lord—brought them none of those things. In fact, their testimony earned them the opposite. Most owned nothing, taking on second jobs to support themselves. They emphasized chastity in deed and thought, and pointed to their lives as examples of that—in other words, they weren't claiming apostolic power to build a harem like other cult leaders throughout history have done. Far from obtaining political power or prestige, they were persecuted severely. Eleven of the twelve of them were executed for refusal to back off from their testimony, with the twelfth (John) being plunged into hot oil and then living out his days in exile on a remote island. All went to their deaths joyfully, claiming it was worth it because they had seen Jesus risen from the dead and they knew eternity with him was better than anything they had given up for him. Does that sound to you like a group who have conspired together to lie? Does it really make sense to think that they all were willing to give up so much, and then to be killed, for something that they *knew* was a lie?

This rag-tag group of poor, uneducated men and their early followers went on to convince half the Roman Empire to believe in Christ's resurrection. Something happened that overturned an empire, shook the world, and redirected the course of history.

Along with many other scholars, I find that alternative explanations for how Christianity got started seem far less compelling than the one the earliest Christians themselves provided as the reason for their behavior: Jesus actually rose from the dead.[23]

THE REAL AND THE COUNTERFEIT

Before I end this interlude, it may help to contrast the evidence for the resurrection with the miraculous claims of another religion, so you can see how truly unique early Christian testimony was. Religious leaders using claims of miraculous powers to beef up their authority is, as you might imagine, quite common in history. But the Christian claims for the Resurrection are of a different nature, and sometimes it's easier to see the quality of the genuine by looking at a counterfeit.

For example, consider the claims of Joseph Smith, the founder of Mormonism. He claimed, in September of 1823, to have found a set of golden plates, with the assistance of an angel, which revealed the essential truths of Mormon doctrine. He later translated what he'd seen, which became, in essence, the Book of Mormon. Eight others claimed to have seen Joseph with the plates, even signing legal affidavits to that effect. Their claims made them quite unpopular in parts of America, and they had to flee for their lives.

On the surface, this seems similar to the claim that Jesus rose from the dead—multiple witnesses testifying to

---

23 If you really want to press into this question, I suggest you get N.T. Wright's *The Resurrection of the Son of God* (Fortress Press, 2003) and dive in. It's very compelling.

something at great personal cost to themselves. But let's dig just a bit.

The eight witnesses claimed to see the golden plates *in a vision, not physically*. Three of them—Oliver Cowdery, David Whitmer, and Martin Harris—who couldn't see the plates, were told that it was only by faith that they would obtain a view. When they finally did "see" them, these three witnesses were not in the room where Smith had supposedly been translating the plates but out in the woods alone, fasting and waiting for the vision. There, they asked God for a vision of the plates through fervent and humble prayer. When praying did not result in the manifestation of the plates, one man, Martin Harris, excused himself (he assumed he was the problem), and the three remaining men continued to pray. Eventually they saw an angel holding the plates.

Later on, Joseph Smith held a special prayer session for Harris, who finally "saw" the plates. And some time later, eight *other* men, through similar processes, said they saw the plates—again, only in a vision.

This bears virtually no similarity to the apostles' claims to see Jesus. They claimed to have seen Jesus not in a vision but in the flesh and to have touched him physically and eaten with him. Unlike the Mormon brethren, most were not *seeking* this revelation, and many did not believe when they first saw him! Most were on their way somewhere, or fleeing for their lives, or hiding together in a room not looking for Jesus when he surprised them. Some of Jesus' appearances happened unexpectedly to large groups at once.

One final distinction between the apostles' claims of the resurrection and Mormon claims of the golden plates: many if not all of the original Mormon witnesses, except Joseph Smith, left the Mormon religion. Some were excommunicated. Others left the faith voluntarily, claiming they had produced their stories under pressure (which is exactly what you might suspect if a miracle claim was exaggerated or fabricated).[24] Joseph Smith's claims brought great personal benefit to him—he was a demigod in the Mormon community, and he used divine "authority" to introduce the practice of polygamy for his own pleasure.

There's an old saying attributed to the 17th-century philosopher Blaise Pascal: "I believe witnesses who get their throats cut." This is where the apostles and the founders of Mormonism part ways. The latter abandoned their faith. The former remained faithful to the end— and the end for them was nearly always that of a violent, shameful death.

A TRUTH TO STAKE YOUR LIFE ON

Other books lay out the evidence of the resurrection in far more thorough and compelling ways than I have been able to in this short interlude. If you want to read more, the research is out there. My goal here is simply to point out how central the belief that Jesus physically rose from the dead is to Christianity—that from the beginning Christians have based their hope on historical fact and not hopeful wishes—and to show you that the evidence *for* the resurrection is stronger than you might have realized.

---

24 J. Warner Wallace, "The Witnesses Of The Resurrection Compared To The Witnesses Of The Golden Plates," April 4, 2013. https://coldcasechristianity.com/writings/the-witnesses-of-the-resurrection-compared-to-the-witnesses-of-the-golden-plates/ (accessed July 18, 2022).

For now, let me just say that I think the German historian and theologian Wolfhart Pannenberg hit the nail on the head when he said, "The evidence for Jesus' resurrection is so strong that nobody would question it except for two things: First, it is a very unusual event. And second, if you believe it happened, you have to change the way you live."

For many people, it's that last thing—that if it's true, they'd have to change the way they live—that holds them up. Remember how we saw in chapter 3 that some people are motivated to suppress the truth? That may be at play again here too. Some don't look deeply at the evidence for the resurrection because they don't care if it's true. In fact, truth be told, they *don't want* it to be true.

But for those open to the existence of God and his work in history, and ready to follow him, the evidence is there, and it is very compelling.

Jesus is alive—literally, physically, actually alive. And because of that, Paul says in Romans, we know he is "the Son of God with power … Jesus Christ our Lord." If he rose from the dead, then he is who says he is, did what he said he did, and can do for you and me what he says he can do. So, let's get back to that.

INCLUSION

Aren't All Religions Basically the Same?

"Then what becomes of our boasting? It is excluded."
(Romans 3:27)

There were only two other people in the boarding area for the late-night flight from Ft. Lauderdale to Charlotte, North Carolina. One was an elderly man who looked at least 80; the other, a beautiful young woman in her early twenties. At the time I was young and single, so I found my feet leading me to sit next to the young woman.

Her name was Berta, and she was from Chile. She was on her way back to Harvard University. I had just graduated from Campbell University, so immediately I felt like we had a connection.[25]

As happens on airplane journeys, we started chatting about what we were doing with our lives, and I told her how Jesus had changed my life, and how I now wanted to spend the rest of my life telling other people about him.

---

25 Harvard, as most people worldwide know, is one of the top colleges in the US. And Campbell... well, Campbell isn't, but those of us who went there should love it dearly: "The Harvard of the Sandhills," as it is affectionately called, only by those who went there.

Berta looked at me with her deep, brooding eyes and said, "You know, at Harvard I am around some of the most driven, intelligent men in the world. But I don't think I've ever heard any of them speak about life with such conviction and purpose... and I find that deeply attractive."

I thought, "This is awesome! Berta's going to put her faith in Jesus, and then we're going to get married. I am going to love telling this story when people say to me, 'So, J.D., how did you and Berta meet?'"

We carried on talking about Jesus for the entire journey. As we began our descent into Charlotte, I thought I had better close the deal (um, for Jesus). So I said, "Berta, would you like to receive Jesus as your Savior?"

Without giving it much thought, she said, "No... you know, that kind of stuff has just never worked for me. I am so happy that you have found your peace in Jesus, but I relate to my God in a different way."

"But, Berta," I said. "Jesus said in John 14:6 that he was the only way to come to God. He provided a salvation for us that we could not provide for ourselves. He's not just my way, Berta; he's the only way."

"Surely you are not saying that there's only one way to come to God?" she answered.

I affirmed that that was indeed exactly what I was saying. I even pointed down at the Gospel of John I was reading from.

"That has to be the most arrogant, closed-minded thing I've ever heard someone say. I can't believe anyone today would be so bigoted as to think that there was only one way to God."

I sat there, unsure of what to say next and mentally unwinding the wedding plans. And then, as the pilot announced our final descent into Charlotte, I had an idea for how to respond.

"Berta," I said, "I sure am glad the pilot of this airplane doesn't look at the airport the way that you do truth."

"What do you mean?"

"Say he announces just now, 'You know, I am sick of that arrogant little control tower always telling me I've got to land this 737 on their favorite little narrow strip of cement. That's their way, not mine. I am an open-minded pilot, so today I am going to attempt to land this aircraft nose first on the tip of the Bank of America building downtown.'"

She said, "That's not a fair comparison."

I said, "Yes, it is. And that's Campbell University, 1; Harvard, 0, by the way, if you're keeping score."[26]

As the words came out of my mouth, I knew that I was not heeding the apostle Peter's instruction to answer those who ask you about your faith "with gentleness and respect" (1 Peter 3:15). I also knew for sure that the wedding was off. Ever since, I've hoped that my brashness didn't create another obstacle in her heart to hearing the Christian message. But still, I stand by that comparison.

Let me go ahead and acknowledge the elephant in the room: Christianity is exclusive. That's because the salvation that Christ offers is a real thing—no less real

---

26 I first told this story in my book *Not God Enough* (Zondervan, 2018), p 96-98.

than the concrete runway that Charlotte airport lays out for incoming planes. A very real God became a very real man and died on a very real cross to pay for your very real sins and rose from a very real grave to reverse the very real curse of death going on in your very real soul. Christianity is not a subjective preference or strategy for self-improvement. It's a real rescue offered to real people with a real problem.

Like my friend Berta, many people today bristle at that claim. Exclusive claims, they say, lead to division, pride, judgmentalism, and even violence, and our world would be better off without them. So believe anything you want; just don't say your way of salvation is the only way...

In this chapter I want to argue that *all* religious claims, even secular ones, are *inherently* exclusive. The gospel, however, is different. Its exclusivity, unlike that of other worldviews, leads to inclusion, not exclusion. That's the point Paul makes at the end of Romans 3.[27]

Confused? Let me explain.

AREN'T WE ALL A LITTLE... EXCLUSIVE?

You might think that an approach that accepts all views about God is broad-minded. Ultimately, however, that view is as exclusive as any other. The Christian theologian Lesslie Newbigin, who served for 40 years as a missionary to India, demonstrated that by pointing out the problem in an Indian parable used to make the all-religions-are-equal point.

---

27 I want to acknowledge my indebtedness to Tim Keller for the layout of this concept through numerous sermons I've heard him preach in which this was a theme.

The parable goes like this. Several blind men fall into a pit with an elephant, at which point they begin to argue about what they've encountered. Grabbing a tusk, one says, "It's a spear." Grabbing the tail, another says, "No, it's a rope." Feeling the elephant's side, still another says, "It's a wall." The last takes hold of an ear, claiming, "It's a fan." The lesson: we're the blind men groping in the dark, and God is the elephant. We've got to stop being so narrow-minded and dogmatic and open up our minds a little bit.

The problem, as Newbigin explains, is that the narrator of this parable claims for herself the very thing that she denies to others: namely, the perspective that sees the whole elephant.[28] The only way she knows that each of the blind men only sees a part is because *she* sees the whole thing. Claiming the very thing for yourself that you forbid to others is, well, a bit unfair.

In the same way, saying that all good people, regardless of their religion, go to heaven sounds broad-minded (#coexist!), but that statement is also sneakily exclusive. After all, if all "good" people go to heaven, haven't you just *excluded* people who are not "good"? And who gets to define what is "good"? Well, I guess *you* do, and I'm guessing your list of "good people" doesn't include those who eat their enemies or kill their children (even though both things have been celebrated in various cultures throughout history). Whatever standard you

---

28 "If the king [who tells this story] were also blind there would be no story. The story is told by the king, and it is the immensely arrogant claim of one who sees the full truth which all the world's religions are only groping after. It embodies the claim to know the full reality which relativizes all the claims of the religions and philosophies." *The Gospel in a Pluralist Society* (Eerdmans, 1989), p 9-10.

set, some are "in" and some are "out." Maybe your list of "good" people excludes those who judge others. Maybe it excludes those in the LGBTQIA+ community, or maybe it's those with an NRA[29] sticker on their back windshield. The point is: all viewpoints end up being exclusive.

The gospel, however, creates an *inclusive* exclusiveness.[30] Let me explain.

AN INCLUSIVE EXCLUSIVENESS

Religious worldviews put us in conflict with others because we are always competing with them to establish ourselves as part of the "good" community. The gospel, however, says that we are saved not because of our inherent goodness, our culture, or even our viewpoints; we are saved by a Christ who died for *all* who would simply receive him. Salvation is a gift, received entirely by grace.

"Then what becomes of our boasting?" Paul asks (Romans 3:27)—of a sense of superiority or attitude of moral condescension? "It is *excluded*," he answers. Why? Because "a person is justified by faith apart from the works of the law." If you know you are not saved by anything you did, then there's nothing to brag about before others. As the old hymn puts it:

> When I survey the wondrous cross,
> On which the prince of glory died,
> My richest gain I count but loss
> And pour contempt on all my pride.[31]

---

29 National Rifle Association.
30 I owe this particular little turn of phrase to Tim Keller.
31 Isaac Watts (1707).

Let me put that into the less-poetic vernacular: the cross makes pride look stupid. On the only report card that really matters, I got a Fail. It's impossible to simultaneously look up to the cross where Jesus had to die for my sins and look down on others for theirs.

There's only one kind of sinner (hopelessly doomed) and only one way of salvation (the wondrous cross)—and thus "one God who will justify the circumcised [religious people] by faith and the uncircumcised [non-religious people] through faith" (v 30). This makes discrimination, Paul says, impossible. At the foot of the cross, the old saying goes, the ground is level. We were *all* "out," and the gospel offers *all* a chance to be "in," not based on their goodness but on his generosity. Our acceptance is based on what was in him, not on what was in us.

Thus, Christianity's uniqueness lies not in its exclusivity but in its *inclusivity*. All worldviews are exclusive, but Christianity's is a viewpoint that leads to radical inclusion. Tim Keller puts it like this: "All religions are exclusive, but Christianity is the most inclusive exclusivity that there is." And if we study church history, we see that what has made the gospel scandalous across the centuries was not whom it excluded but whom it included. Go check it out.

Nearly 150 years ago, the British pastor C.H. Spurgeon identified three types of pride causing societal divisions in Britain that were upended by the gospel. These observations are as relevant in today's West as they were then.

The Pride of Race

Many take pride in their ethnic or cultural or national identity. In Paul's day, Jews took pride in their Jewishness and Romans took pride in their Romanness; today it might be in our "whiteness," "blackness," "Americanness," Hispanic origin or European descent, or whatever. There is nothing wrong with taking delight in our cultures—it's quite appropriate, in fact, as God created our various cultures as a kaleidoscope of his glory. The problem comes when culture becomes our primary identity—something that sets us apart from others.

When that happens, the results are division and racial strife. Each culture becomes focused on defending its honor or its purity.

The gospel eliminates this boasting by teaching that there's truly only one race of people (human) sharing one common problem (sin) with one hope (Jesus).

Paul understood this one firsthand. Perhaps no ethnic group in history has felt more pride in their ethnicity than 1st-century Jews. Jews, on the one hand, had been chosen among all ethnicities to receive the revelation of God. All God's prophets had come from them, and much of their culture was formed by the direct command of God. On the other hand, they were a beleaguered and oppressed people, which gave them solidarity in the face of Roman dominance. This, understandably, gave Jewish people a lot of pride in their heritage, and their historical identity was something they fell back on in the face of oppression.

Yet Paul, who had grown up loving his Jewishness, said that in comparison to his identity in Christ, his Jewishness was like "rubbish" to him (Philippians 3:8). "Rubbish" is actually too gentle a translation there—the Greek word is *scubala,* and scholars say it's the kind of word that, if you heard one of your kids use it, you would wash out their mouth with soap! It's not that Paul stopped appreciating his Jewishness—just that compared to the worth of knowing Jesus, it became far less important. It was like comparing a Timex watch with a Rolex.

When we put our faith in Jesus, our cultural distinctives do not go away, nor do we need to downplay or deny them. Our preferences and historically-shaped perspectives are like the faces of a diamond that God uses to display his glory. God is not telling Jewish people to act like Gentiles or Gentiles to become Jews, or black believers to act like white believers. He's telling all of us to identify *first and foremost* as "kingdom people," regarding our cultural heritage as of distant secondary importance.

I'm painfully aware that Christians have often not lived up to these ideals. My own "tribe" (Americans of European descent) did lasting damage to our society by denying those of different ethnic descent the freedoms we demanded for ourselves. And sadly, some of our Christian forebears used Bible passages to justify their bigotry. They did this, however, not *because* of the gospel they believed but *despite* it. It's not that they took the Bible too literally; it's that they overlooked the sections that were inconvenient.

The Pride of Face

The "pride of face" comes from thinking that our beauty, talent, wealth, and accomplishments set us apart from others. We assume that we are solely to credit for these things. The beautiful girl does not merely happen to look better than her neighbor; her beauty means she *is* better. The accomplished business leader did not merely take advantage of talents and opportunities bestowed by God;

he became who he was because of an inherent superiority that he had over others.

Any circumspect reflection on our accomplishments, however, has to recognize the role that benefits we had no part in choosing played in our successes. Your talents were inherited from your parents—genetics that you had no choice in. You played little part in the health you enjoyed or the social constructs that enabled you to prosper. I'm not taking away from the hard work you put in to get yourself where you are—I'm just saying there is a lot we take for granted. Do we really think we'd have accomplished all that we have if we'd been born a special-needs orphan in a village in Somalia? There are no grounds for pride here, but only gratitude.

Even more importantly, our earthly accomplishments—even the ones we worked the hardest for and feel the greatest satisfaction in—carry *no* weight in overcoming the one obstacle that really matters: obtaining eternal life. For gaining favor with God, the best of the best of our accomplishments are (to use Paul's term) *scubala*.

The Pride of Grace

The most insidious version of pride, Spurgeon said, is the pride of grace—the belief that our *religious* accomplishment makes us better than others. If there's ever been a contradiction in terms, "pride of grace" is it—but our hearts quickly and effortlessly turn there.

The Bible teaches that, apart from grace, the best of our good works are like "filthy rags" to God (Isaiah 64:6). The word Isaiah uses for filthy rags means "diseased" or "defiled," such as the rag a leper would use to bind his or her open wound. Imagine standing before God and he asks you why he should let you into his kingdom, and you put down in front of him a pile of disease-ridden, blood- and pus-filled rags. The best of our righteous deeds, Isaiah says, are like those filthy rags—still saturated and stained with sin. It's like Paul said in Romans 3: "None is righteous, no, not one ... for all have sinned, and fall short of the glory of God" (v 10, 23).

The whole point of the gospel is that, in Christ, God gives us what we don't deserve. We stand right with God not because of a righteousness we achieved but because of a righteousness given to us in Christ.

If you are a Christian, it's not because you were a better person than someone else. You didn't discover the truth about Christ because you were more logical or more historically savvy. Paul says that none of us can even recognize the Lordship of Jesus unless we are empowered by the Holy Spirit (1 Corinthians 12:3). It was God, Paul explained to the Philippians, who gave us both the desire *and* the ability to follow Jesus (Philippians 2:13). From start to finish, the Christian's journey is one of grace. There's no room for pride here—only humble gratitude.

A Christian's entire hope is based on grace. What distinguishes us is not our ethnicity, our accomplishments, or our good deeds. It's grace, grace, grace. So what becomes of our boasting, our pride, our divisiveness, then? It is all *excluded*.

CAESAR VS. JESUS

Ours is not the first society to value inclusiveness. Rome was all about religious inclusivism. Historians say that Rome essentially had only one basic religious rule: don't say your god is the only one. Worship any god you want, but don't claim yours is the only one, because, they reasoned, if you do, you will start to think you should be in charge. Worship any god you want, but let Rome make the rules—they are the narrator who sees the whole elephant. The 2nd-century Roman emperor Hadrian built the Pantheon, which housed gods from all over the Roman Empire, showing that they all had a place in his empire. Rome was the eternal city, where Caesar was regarded as "the Son of God, the King of Kings and Lord of Lords."[32]

Some Christian traditions claim that early in Christianity's history, one of the Caesars, attempting to make peace with Christians, offered to put a statue of Jesus in the Pantheon. You might imagine that Christians would have been honored—"What? Little old us, who started in a backwoods corner of the little province of Judea, recognized officially by Rome? Our guy in the hall of fame! What an honor!"

You'd be wrong. They said that Jesus could never stand as one god among many—one way of salvation amid a buffet of others. At the cost of their lives, they maintained that no one else was worthy of worship and that salvation was found in no one else, but only in "one name under heaven given among men, whereby we must be saved" (Acts 4:12).

Did their belief lead them into divisiveness, strife, and superiority? Quite the opposite. The Baylor sociologist Rodney Stark claims that one of the reasons why

32 Clifford Ando, *Imperial Rome AD 193 to 284: The Critical Century* (Edinburgh University Press, 2012), https://www.newworldencyclopedia.org/entry/Son_of_God (accessed July 7, 2022).

Christianity grew so quickly in the Roman Empire was that their congregations were the *only* places in the entire empire where different classes, races, and cultures could come together and sit down in harmony.[33] Part of Rome's "civilizing" project was to bring masses of people from different cultures to live together in large urban areas. But living together only heightened ethnic strife, social hierarchies, and cultural tension. In Christian churches, however, former enemies learned to forgive. Societal adversaries sat down as brothers and sisters. Priests and former prostitutes sat on level ground at the foot of the cross. Rome's "inclusiveness" led to iron-fisted control, persecution, and ghettoed segregation. Meanwhile, the gospel, underneath Rome's iron fist, created the most inclusive community the world had ever seen.

The gospel is doing the same thing today. Skeptics try to write off Christianity as only a white, middle-class, Western religion. The truth is that Christianity originated as a Middle Eastern movement and is now growing the fastest among Latin American, African, and Asian peoples. Historian Mark Noll notes in his book *The New Shape of World Christianity* that on any given Sunday...

- more Christians attend church in Kenya than do in Canada.

---

33 "Christianity revitalized life in Greco-Roman cities by providing new norms and new kinds of social relationships able to cope with many urgent urban problems. To cities filled with the homeless and impoverished, Christianity offered charity as well as hope. To cities filled with newcomers and strangers, Christianity offered an immediate basis for attachments. To cities filled with orphans and widows, Christianity provided a new and expanded sense of family. To cities torn by violent ethnic strife, Christian offered a new basis for social solidarity." *The Rise of Christianity* (Princeton University Press, 1996), p 161.

- each of Uganda, Kenya, Tanzania, and Nigeria have more Anglicans than Britain, Canada, and the United States combined.

- this past Sunday there were more Presbyterians at church in Ghana than in Scotland.

- Brazil now sends more overseas missionaries than does Britain or Canada.

- in 1970 there were no legally functioning churches in all of China. But it is estimated that today the number of practicing Christians in China exceeds the number in the United States.

- the largest church in Korea has more people present for a single worship service than are at Canada's ten largest churches combined.

And Rome? For all their talk of inclusion, Rome became one of the bloodiest, cruelest, most imperialistic dynasties in history. They had to maintain their role as "parable narrator" by the edge of a sword.

Christianity offers a uniquely inclusive exclusivism. I may differ from another Christian in many ways—we may appreciate different things and bring different perspectives to a whole host of questions—but we are bound by two things in the deepest part of our identity: first, we are both sinners against God, and second, we are both saved by the God-Man from Nazareth. That destroys pride and division and unites us in humility.

What about you? What is your "boast"? If it's not the gospel, it will lead to division. If it is the gospel, and you let its truth take root deep in your heart, you'll find you can't help but genuinely welcome in the outsider.

The cross yields a radical inclusiveness that welcomes anyone, celebrates everyone, and looks down on no one.

Which, Berta, if you're reading this, is what I wish I'd said to you as we taxied down the narrow strip of runway at Charlotte airport.

STRUGGLE

Why Does the Christian Life Seem So Hard?

"For I do not do the good I want, but the evil I do not want is what I keep on doing." (Romans 7:19)

Dr. Jekyll, in Robert Louis Stevenson's famous novel, is a fine, upstanding citizen who is frustrated because he feels that inside of him there exists "a sort of duality"—a bad part and a good part, with the bad part of him always holding back the good part. So he develops a potion that separates his two parts. Only the good part, the "Dr. Jekyll," comes out by day, and only the bad part, Mr. Hyde (short for "Mr. Hideous"), comes out at night. Each now exists unrestrained by the other.

The problem is that the evil part of Dr. Jekyll is far more evil than he had ever imagined. Mr. Hyde's every thought is centered on himself. He is spiteful and hateful, driven by murderous rage. "I was tenfold more wicked than I ever thought," says Dr. Jekyll. Stevenson concludes...

"Man is not truly one, but truly two ... Of the two natures that contended in the field of my consciousness,

even if I could rightly be said to be either, it was only because I was radically both." [34]

I'm not sure if Stevenson's story was inspired by Romans chapter 7, but that's how the apostle Paul describes himself:

"For I do not do the good I want, but the evil I do not want is what I keep on doing. Now if I do what I do not want, it is no longer I who do it, but sin that dwells within me. So I find it to be a law that when I want to do right, evil lies close at hand." (Romans 7:19-21)

MY DISAPPOINTING CHRISTIAN LIFE

Lots of Christians have a life verse—a verse that encapsulates what they've experienced with God so far and what they aspire to be. Things like "We know that for those who love God all things work together for good" (Romans 8:28) or "I can do all things through him who strengthens me" (Philippians 4:13).

If I were honest, Romans 7:19 might fit best as mine. You could sum up my life as "so many good intentions, so little progress." I've been a Christian for over 30 years now, and I am often dismayed at my lack of spiritual maturity. Why do I still struggle so much with self-control? Why am I still so instinctively jealous over the successes of others? Why am I so tightfisted with money, even money I don't really need? Why does gossip come so much more naturally to me than prayer?

---

34 *The Strange Case of Dr. Jekyll and Mr. Hyde* (1886), p 108. https://en.wikisource.org/wiki/Page:Stevenson_-_Strange_case_of_Dr._Jekyll_and_Mr._Hyde_(1886).djvu/118 (accessed July 7, 2022).

Paul's Romans 7 confession feels like a lifeline to me because in it I see that even for him, the great apostle, the Christian life was not one easy victory after another. Quite the opposite. It's vital to get our minds around that. Otherwise, soon enough, we'll get discouraged and think, "Something didn't take. I must be not cut out for this Christianity thing. Or maybe it's not even real."

The "normal" Christian life is a struggle, to the very end. Though your sins are forgiven, your future perfection is assured, and God's Spirit is at work in you (as we'll see in the next chapter), you still carry around with you a sinful nature in the "members" (or parts) of your body (v 23)—your "Mr. Hyde"—that is as bad as it's always been.

Here's how Paul described his heart:

> "For I do not understand what I am doing ... I do not
> practice what I want to do, but I do what I hate ...
> I know that nothing good lives in me, that is, in my
> flesh. For the desire to do what is good is with me, but
> there is no ability to do it." (Romans 7:15, 18, CSB)

Paul is talking as if there are two of him—there's the "him" that wants to do good and the other "him" that does the exact opposite. There's his "flesh" self—that is, his sinful nature, the "him" that existed *before* Jesus rescued him—and then there's his new self, who loves Jesus and wants to obey him. Since there is no potion that can quarantine each part from the other, they struggle against each other all day every day.

Tim Keller describes Paul's feelings in Romans 7 as like a man struggling in a battle that it seems he can't win when in reality he's in a battle he can't lose. And therein lies hope. It's an amazing truth, so buckle up.

THE BATTLE WE CAN'T WIN

The battle Paul feels that he can't win is the battle to bring his bodily "members" into submission to God's law. *Trying to force myself to do what's right*, Paul laments, *just reveals how much I want to do the opposite. Making myself obey isn't changing my heart; if anything, it is arousing more sinful passions in me.*

Paul then anticipates the objection of his Jewish readers: *Are you saying God's law is bad, Paul? Why are you always so hard on the law?! It's almost like you're saying we'd be better off without it!*

Paul responds, *Absolutely not!* "Yet if it had not been for the law, I would not have known sin." *The law reveals to us how sinful we are. It is like a mirror we look into that shows us how far short we have fallen of what God wants!*

To drive the point home, he uses as an example the tenth commandment: "For I would not have known what it is to covet if the law had not said, 'You shall not covet'" (v 7).

To covet is to desperately desire what somebody else has, because you are unsatisfied with what God has given to you. *God's law*, Paul says, *told me that a righteous heart, a healthy heart, is a heart that doesn't covet. But my whole life I've yearned for the experiences, talents, and achievements of others, feeling jealous of their families, reputations, and riches.*

Up until that wrestling with that command, Paul had thought of himself as a pretty good person. He'd never committed adultery, stolen money, killed anyone, or bowed down to pagan statues. But that tenth commandment, "You shall not covet," cut him straight to the heart.

Obedience to that tenth and final commandment, you see, has nothing to do with *external* conformity to a set of laws. It's about our *internal* attitude toward others. And Paul knew that he was envious of others. That coveting spirit, he came to understand, is actually behind disobedience to some of the other commandments. For example:

- Why does someone steal? They steal because they covet what someone else has. Paul may not have stolen, but he'd coveted others' belongings.

- Why does someone lie? Quite often, it is because they covet something that they can't get with the truth, so they twist the truth to get it. They exaggerate certain things or minimize their faults to gain approval. Or they lie to obtain a position or an advantage they couldn't get with the truth. Maybe Paul hadn't told lies, but he had coveted those things.

- Why does someone commit adultery? They covet sex with someone that God hasn't given to them. Paul probably hadn't committed adultery, but he'd fantasized about sexual pleasure with people he wasn't married to.

Coveting, then, is one of the primary forces at work in our hearts when we disobey. A coveting heart puts us at odds with the entire spirit of the law.

So in that one commandment, Paul saw just how far away he actually was from the heart of God. And that was when the wheels really came off for him. That made sin, in his words, *come alive* in him, because sensing how covetous his heart was just made him *more* insecure with God, which made him even more zealous to show that he was better than others, which made him more competitive, which made him more envious. The commandment, "You shall not covet," far from curing his heart, had the opposite effect. It exposed his heart and, in the process, made it worse!

Imagine you are in bed, sick with the flu, and I show up by your bedside and start to give you commands that would be no problem for a healthy person: "Straighten up your room. Do a little exercise. Stop coughing. Don't run a fever." These are all things a healthy person would do easily—naturally, even. Yet for a sick person, the harder they tried to keep those "laws," the worse they'd get.

All this brought Paul to the realization that no law, no command, no iron-clad resolution could fix him. The battle to conform his heart to the law was a battle he *couldn't* win. That drove him to look to the gospel, where he discovered a battle he couldn't lose.

THE BATTLE WE CAN'T LOSE

The gospel transformed the battlefront for Paul. Because the gospel is primarily an announcement of the victory that *Jesus* had won for his people, not a summons to fight a battle for him, the battle changed from one Paul couldn't win to one he couldn't lose. Christ had won the victory, and by faith Christ's victory was now Paul's. In Christ, Paul was a new creation.

That didn't mean his old nature was gone, though:

> "For we know that the law is spiritual, but I am of the flesh, sold under sin. For I do not understand my own actions. For I do not do what I want, but I do the very thing I hate." (Romans 7:14-15)

> "*For I have the desire to do what is right, but not the ability to carry it out.*" (Romans 7:18)

> "*So I find it to be a law that when I want to do right, evil lies close at hand.*" (Romans 7:21)

Paul, in these verses, is not describing his pre-conversion self, but his present, committed-Christian-and-apostle self. Notice all the present-tense verbs. Paul says, "I *have* the desire to do what is right." Have—present tense. Paul is justified, redeemed, and resurrected in Christ, but still his old sinful nature resists his every good intention. And Paul knows that the moment he ignores Mr. Hyde, Mr. Hyde is going to ruin him.

But at the same time, Paul knows that in Christ he has ultimate victory. Jesus had declared "It is finished" over Paul's salvation, paying the full price for his sin on the cross and overcoming all its powers in the resurrection. Understanding that reality changed Paul's disposition in the fight. He says, *I know my sinful cravings are not the true "me" anymore. It's the old me, the dead me—not the renewed me in Christ.*

I remember hearing a story about a married guy—we'll call him Jack—who was a philanderer. When he became a Christian, he turned away from his adulterous lifestyle. Shortly after, he was on a business trip, and in the hotel a woman he'd previously had an affair with came up to him. He tried to politely walk away. The woman grew more insistent and said, "Jack, what are you doing? Come on, it's me! It's me!" He replied, "I know. But it's not *me* anymore."

In Christ we are new creations. While we still possess the old flesh, with all its sinful attractions, inside is a new us, renewed in Christ.

Here's why that change of thinking is important. When, as a Christian, you fall back into an old, sinful habit, you're going to start beating yourself up, saying, "See, nothing has changed. I still desire the same old sins. I'll *never* get better." But that's wrong—the truth is that you're now in a battle you can't lose, because Jesus has already won it. There is a new you. You will still struggle with sin—you will still sometime succumb to that insidious Mr. Hyde—but your future victory is certain.

December 1941 was a dark time for Great Britain. World War II was not going well, and the nation lived with the constant fear of a German invasion. But on the morning of Sunday, December 7, when Germany's ally, Japan, attacked Pearl Harbor, U.S. President Franklin Roosevelt told British Prime Minister Winston Churchill, "We are all in the same boat now." Churchill later wrote in his memoir, "No American will think it wrong of me to proclaim that hearing the U.S. was on our side was the greatest joy to me. England would live. Britain would live. The rest of the war would simply be about the proper allocating of overwhelming force. I went to bed that night and slept the sleep of the saved and the thankful." Confidence that "overwhelming force" had joined his side transformed Churchill's attitude from despair to hope. Nothing in the war had tangibly changed—Hitler was still on the offensive—but Churchill rested in the assurance of victory that came from the promise of overwhelming force.

The finished work of Christ, the resurrection, and the gift of the Holy Spirit are the "overwhelming forces" promised to us in salvation. So, although Paul laments, "What a wretched man I am! Who will rescue me from this body of death?" he can immediately rejoice in the answer: "Thanks be to God through Jesus Christ our Lord!" (Romans 7:24, CSB).

MAKING THE TRANSITION

So, the question is: how does the Christian, on a day-by-day basis, go from feeling like they are in a battle they can't win to fighting with hope in a battle they can't lose?

We'll more fully unpack the answer to that question in our next chapter, but let me give you a little teaser here: we experience the victory of the gospel by every day re-believing the news of Christ's victory.

In chapter 6 of the book of Romans, Paul tells the struggling believer:

> *"Likewise you also, reckon yourselves to be dead indeed to sin, but alive to God in Christ Jesus our Lord."*
> *(Romans 6:11, NKJV)*

"Reckon" is that Greek word Paul has used before: *logizomai* (4:5). In chapter 6 of this book, we saw that it meant "credited." Paul explained that when we first trusted God's promise to remove our sin, God *credited* our faith as righteousness. It's an accounting term; it means to look at one thing and consider it to be another.

Well, now, Paul says, *it's our turn to do the crediting— the counting, or reckoning.* We are to reckon ourselves as already dead to sin, even though sin still feels very much alive in us. As we do, God infuses the power of new life into us. Literally, by believing you are in the resurrection, God infuses into you the power of resurrection. Paul is not talking about a mental trick or the power of positive thinking: God releases resurrection power—the power to live the Christian life—into us as we re-believe the gospel. In Christianity, believing is the way to becoming.

That's why I said, back in chapter 1, that the gospel is not just the beginning point of Christianity—the diving board off of which you jump into the pool. The gospel is the pool itself. Just as faith in the finished work of Christ obtained for us the release from the penalty of sin, so continued faith in it releases us from sin's power. To progress in the Christian life is always, as Luther said, *to begin again*—to go back to the essentials of the gospel. The gospel is the place from which all the Christian's power flows.

LET THE STRUGGLE TAKE YOU DEEPER

Perhaps you're asking: But why does it have to be this way? Why does God leave his followers to struggle with sin? Why wouldn't God just immediately cure us of Mr. Hyde?

Good question, and I'm not sure I know the full answer. One thing we can be sure of, however, is that God uses our ongoing struggle against the flesh to deepen our appreciation for his grace, just as he did with Paul. Maybe the only way we'll ever learn to exclaim, "Who will deliver me from this body of death? Thanks be to God through Jesus Christ our Lord!" is by realizing, first-hand, just how thoroughly sin has ruined us and how powerless we are, in ourselves, to live a successful Christian life.

Jesus said that only those who have been forgiven much, love much (Luke 7:47). That means God uses our ongoing struggle with sin to drive us more deeply into grace, which deepens our love for Jesus. Awareness of the depth of the love of God for us is what produces passionate love for God in us.

C.S. Lewis said that it seemed to him that God sometimes lets us struggle with lesser sins to keep us from the greatest ones—pride, complacency, and apathy. If we never struggled with sin, we might forget how desperate we are for God's grace and how dependent we are on his Spirit.

Back at the end of the eighteenth century, when John Newton, the writer of the famous hymn "Amazing Grace," was in his eighties, he wrote in a letter to a friend in which he confessed that he had always assumed that by then, after walking with God for over 50 years, he'd have achieved complete victory over his temptations. Some of them, however, felt stronger to him than ever. "Is something wrong with my spirituality?" he asked (I'm paraphrasing). "Am I not really saved?"

He had come to realize, he said, that God let him struggle with these temptations to keep him closely tethered to grace.[35] This side of the resurrection, true growth in grace, he said, doesn't mean getting to a place where

---

35 This is a common theme in Newton's letters. Here is one of the more concise quotes capturing the idea: "The unchangeableness of the Lord's love, and the riches of his mercy, are likewise more illustrated by the multiplied pardons he bestows upon his people, than if they needed no forgiveness at all. Hereby the Lord Jesus Christ is more endeared to the soul; all boasting is effectually excluded, and the glory of a full and free salvation is ascribed to him alone." "Advantages from Remaining Sin," in *Letters of John Newton* (Banner of Truth, 1976), p 133. See also his letters entitled "Causes, Nature, and Marks of a Decline in Grace," "Believer's Inability on Account of Remaining Sin," and "Contrary Principles in the Believer," within the same volume.

you no longer feel you need God's grace, but growing in your awareness of just how desperate for that grace you actually are.

Only when we lament with Paul, "Wretched man [or woman] that I am!" will we sing with John Newton, "Amazing grace, how sweet the sound, that saved a wretch like me."

I'm quite confident that if I didn't struggle with some persistent, ongoing sinful tendencies, my sinful heart would conclude that I was really good at obeying Jesus. Ironic as it sounds, I would grow proud of my obedience, and that would make me worse than ever. Uggg! I hate that Mr. Hyde. I can't wait to get to heaven when I can put this sinful struggle behind me. For now, God uses these sinful struggles to grow my gratitude for his grace. My struggle humbles me, but it doesn't leave me in despair. I know God will finish this work he started in me. Simultaneously living in the midst of a battle I can't win while being assured that I'm really in one I can't lose produces in me a humble confidence and a confident humility—which is what God wants.

That is why Paul ends Romans 7 worshipfully, not fearfully. Paul knows he is weak, but he has a Savior who is strong.

And so, with that as a backdrop, Paul turns to introduce us to the power—the overwhelming force—that guarantees our future victory and makes progress toward it possible. This power does not remove the struggle, but it does empower it. It's a power at work in every Christian right now, and it's a power that is arguably the most overlooked resource in the Christian life.

But first, we've got to deal with one more thing that sometimes trips people up as they near the finish line... In thinking about the Christian life as a "struggle," this is the place that many struggle the most—to the point that they wonder, if this kind of struggle is going on inside them, how the Christian account of things could possibly be true.

WHAT ABOUT THE CHRISTIAN VIEW OF SEXUALITY?

Way back in Romans 1, we saw that our rejection of God corrupted every dimension of our lives (Romans 1:24-32). I listed a few areas where we experience that corruption, but those with sharp eyes may have noticed that I skipped the most controversial part of the list. I wasn't ducking it—I wanted to leave it for this place in this book, now that we've thought about the difference faith in Christ makes in our view of who we are and how we should live. For all of us, there's a "new me" that has to be embraced, and an "old me" that needs to be left behind.

Here's the part we didn't go into in chapter 3—the part where Paul talks about one of the ways in which sin affects our sexuality:

"For this reason God gave them up to dishonorable passions. For their women exchanged natural sexual relations for those that are contrary to nature; and the men likewise gave up natural relations with women and were consumed with passion for one another." (Romans 1:26-27)

Maybe Paul's words feel like a conversation-stopper to you. I've heard the Bible's prescriptions on sexuality called a "defeater"—that is, an aspect of a belief system that is so outrageous that it invalidates everything else in that belief system. For many, the Bible's teaching on sexuality does just that.

Before you toss this book aside, at least give me a chance to address three myths that our culture—and far too often our churches—has promoted about the Bible and homosexuality. And then I want to offer a suggestion that has helped me—and scores of people I've known over the years—not get derailed by this in our search for God.

Myth 1: When It Comes to Homosexuality, There Are Only Two Choices: Affirmation or Alienation

Many assume that when someone announces they are gay, our only options are affirmation or alienation, and if we are not doing the former, we must be doing the latter. Not embracing someone's sexual choices, we are told, dismisses them as a person.

Tragically, the church has often embraced that dichotomy. How many heartbreaking stories do we have to hear of parents rejecting gay children, of gay kids bullied by "Christian" friends at school, or of churches ostracizing those struggling with same-sex attraction? Too often, the church has treated the LGBTQIA+ community more like a political adversary to be vanquished than a community to be loved and served.

Jesus took a different approach. He spoke truth, no matter how unpopular or countercultural it was, but he befriended outsiders. He told people hard truth, but only as he drew them close. Unlike us, he did not push away those whose lifestyles he disagreed with. He asked about their problems and ate at their houses. He saw the outcast in his society as individuals made in his Father's image to be valued, befriended, and loved.

Behind this myth is another one: our sexual orientation defines us. "Gay" and "straight" are treated as identities that form the inextricable core of who we are. The gospel teaches something different: every person is first and foremost a man or woman bearing the *imago Dei* (image of God). We cannot reduce anyone (including ourselves) to their choices or desires. Every person is worthy of our respect and compassion because they bear the stamp of our Creator. All of us, alike, have rebelled against our Creator. At the most fundamental level, we're all in the same boat.

Because of that, we do not need to choose between affirmation and alienation. Jesus showed us a third way—grace. That is to say, we recognize that the corruption someone else experiences may be different than the corruption we experience, but that doesn't mean that they are fundamentally different than us. We are both made in the image of God, with the same root problem—sin—and needing the same divine solution—salvation.

That brings us to myth #2.

Myth 2: Homosexuality Is the Worst Sin

Paul lists homosexuality as one of the many fruits of a disordered heart, not the only one. It is an example of doing what I desire rather than what the Creator desires—of seeking to be who I want to be rather than who the Creator has declared me to be, or to pursue relationships differently than he says they should be pursued. Gay relationships share the same "root sins" with all other sins: idolatry and rebellion—substituting my desires for God's and usurping his authority with my will. Those roots are buried deep in the hearts of us all, even if they "flower" in different ways.

In Romans 1, Paul offers multiple examples of that rebellion: things like deceit, boasting, greed, disobedience of our parents, unnatural sexual desires, slander, breaking covenants, and many things. Each of us struggles with certain things on Paul's list more than others, but they are all fruits of the same poisonous roots—idolatry and rebellion.

Let me make clear: homosexuality in and of itself does not send you to hell. Here's how I know that: heterosexuality doesn't send you to heaven. What condemns any of us is refusing to allow Jesus to be the Lord of our lives, regardless of how that rebellion manifests itself—in your sexual life, in what you do with your money, in how you relate to authority, in how you talk to your parents, or in how you talk about your neighbors.

Rosaria Butterfield, formerly a practicing lesbian and professor of Literature and Women's Studies at Syracuse University in New York, recounts her conversion to Christ in her book *The Secret Thoughts of an Unlikely Convert*. She says that Paul's letter to the Romans pushed her to look beyond her sexual desires to the root questions behind them:

Who in my life gets to declare what is good?

> Who or what is Lord in my life—my desires or
> God's word?

She says that homosexuality is not the core of our rebellion against God; a desire to be God—to be the one who gets to declare what is good and what is evil—is. At root, she says, it's about pride: "Proud people always feel that they can live independently from God and from other people. Proud people feel entitled to do what they want when they want to."[36]

Ultimately, Butterfield says, we all come to Christ in the same way—by repenting of (that is, turning away from) our rebellion and putting faith in the finished work of Christ (remember chapter 6).

Becket Cook was a gay man working in Hollywood's entertainment industry when he became a Christian (in part) through a study of the book of Romans. He explains that for his entire life, people had been telling him to be "true to himself." But, he writes, the Bible says that the "self"...

> *"... is corrupted by sin, so why be true to that? The whole idea of this is bound to the exaltation of self. It carries the implication of making yourself your own god. Putting yourself and your desires on a pedestal and worshiping them. Being true to yourself is nothing short of idolatry ... No thank you. I don't want to be true to myself. I want to be true to God and his word."* [37]

Repentance for the LGBTQIA+ person, then, is essentially the same as repentance for a straight person: "God, I'm

---

36 *Secret Thoughts of an Unlikely Convert* (Crown & Covenant Publications, 2014), p 30-31.
37 *A Change of Affection* (Thomas Nelson, 2019), p 120.

sorry for elevating my desires over your will. I'm sorry for attempting to define my identity aside from your design for me. I'm sorry for taking on myself the authority to declare what's good. I'm sorry for seeking satisfaction in self-fulfillment rather than from giving glory to you. I recognize Jesus is Lord and turn over control to him."

The gospel message is not "Let the gay become straight" but "Let the dead become alive."

Myth 3: Being Born with Something Makes It OK

Often we hear this objection: "Most gay people didn't choose to be gay; at some point they discovered they were. It's wrong for God to condemn someone for something they had no choice in."

But it's not as simple as that. Many impulses instinctive to us we recognize as wrong—things like anger, greed, and vengeance. If a shamed man feels that the only way he can restore his honor is through an "honor killing," most of us would say that that is an impulse he should suppress, even if exacting vengeance feels right to him. The point is not that homosexuality is comparable to an honor-killing, but just that mere possession of a desire does not make it right to act upon it.

The Bible never points us to look within for truth. There are some beautiful things in our personal makeup that reflect God's image, but Mr. Hyde also lives in there. We were not born pure. We were all *born* under sin, and because of that, Jesus says, we must all be "born again" (John 3:3). We need a new start and a new heart: a heart that loves what God loves. Trusting Christ as Savior is how we obtain that heart. When we embrace the gospel, our sins are forgiven and we are born again.

But full transformation doesn't happen all at once, as we saw in chapter 8. Christianity is a lifelong struggle of denying our sinful natural desires and trusting Christ for renewal. Persevering in the struggle honors Christ, even as we wait for final redemption (for more on this, see p 158-159).

THE BIBLE IS AN EQUAL-OPPORTUNITY OFFENDER

Paul's letter to the Romans makes it clear: practicing homosexuality is a sinful choice—a departure from God's design. In another letter, Paul says:

> "Neither the sexually immoral, nor idolaters, nor
> adulterers, nor men who have sex with men ... will
> inherit the kingdom of God." (1 Corinthians 6:9-10)

I realize that this is countercultural in the 21st-century West. If it's any consolation, the Bible's sexual ethic has offended almost every culture, though for different reasons. Ancient cultures were offended by the New Testament's emphasis on monogamous marriage, the equality of the sexes, and Jesus' impulse to forgive a female adulterer rather than stone her (John 8:1-11). Of course, we accept most of those as "givens" now. That's why I say the Bible is an equal-opportunity offender. Sam Allberry, a Christian writer and speaker who from his teenage years has experienced same-sex attraction, says it like this in his book *Why Does God Care Who I Sleep With?*:

> "Christian sexual ethics have been countercultural
> in every culture. This is important to understand.
> It is easy to assume that Christian sexual ethics are
> old-fashioned. But that presumes some prior time in

history when the Bible's teaching neatly matched our own sensibilities. But this has never been the case ...

"The teaching of the Bible always ends up critiquing major aspects of any culture's view of sex and marriage, even while affirming other aspects. We might look at the Bible's teaching in horror, exclaiming, 'But it's the Twenty-First Century!' But it's not all that different from someone in the Roman Empire reading [Paul] ... exclaiming 'But this is the First Century!' Though the reasons have varied from age to age and culture to culture, Christian teaching on this issue has never been in vogue." [38]

Paul's approach to homosexuality is neither what we'd call classically liberal nor classically conservative. He doesn't deny homosexuality's sinfulness, nor does he treat it as if it were a fundamentally different kind of sin. He lists homosexuality and gender confusion as one of many manifestations of the corruption that came from humanity's decision to reject God and worship other things in his place.

So, can you be gay and a Christian? Here's Becket Cook again, making a very helpful distinction:

"This one is complex, so let's break it down. First, we must define what we mean by gay. If you mean continuously and unrepentantly engaging in homosexual behavior, then no, you cannot be a gay Christian. But if you mean having a same-sex orientation but not acting on that impulse, then yes, you can be gay and a Christian." [39]

38 *Why Does God Care Who I Sleep With?* (The Good Book Company, 2020), p 63.
39 *A Change of Affection*, p 120.

STILL NOT THERE YET? IT'S OK TO PUNT FOR A WHILE

One reason I wanted to put this Intermission here, rather than after the first couple of chapters, is because (as C.S. Lewis said in *Mere Christianity*) sexual ethics are not the center of the Christian message—Jesus is.[40] Becoming a Christian means surrendering to his Lordship. If he's Lord, you'll probably have a lot of things to rethink. So, to use a metaphor from American football, it's ok to punt on this particular question for a while. Focus on the question of whether Jesus is Lord. If he is, you can work your way outward from there. He'll help you.

I love how Sam Allberry concludes his book:

> "[Christianity] is a message not primarily concerned with what we do and don't do with our genitals (though it has significant things to say about this), but with who we will ultimately give our hearts to, and where we will look for our deepest experience of love." [41]

Christianity is all about Jesus, so we'll end this intermission in his company. Throughout his life, we see him demonstrating great sympathy for those caught in sexual sin. In one incident, he was confronted by a group of religious leaders about to stone an adulterous woman to death. (You can read about it in John 8:3-11.) He did not tell her that her sexual choices were nobody else's business, nor did he write her off as permanently disqualified. His most challenging words were not

---

40 "I want to make it as clear as I possibly can that the centre of Christian morality is not here." *Mere Christianity*, p 94.
41 *Why Does God Care Who I Sleep With?*, p 137.

directed to her but to the men who were judging her. To her, he said words he extends to all who are willing to come in surrender to him:

> *"Neither do I condemn you; go, and from now on sin no more." (John 8:11)*

SPIRIT

What Is the Difference Between Being Religious and Being Spiritual?

"The Spirit of life has set you free in Christ Jesus from the law of sin and death." (Romans 8:2)

The fastest-growing religious category in the US today is "spiritual but not religious."

Increasingly (as we saw in the first chapter), people are turning their backs on religious institutions, but they're not giving up on the idea that life has a spiritual side to it. A survey done within the last several years found that the proportion of Americans describing their outlook as "spiritual but not religious" rose by over 40%, while those who identified as "religious" fell 11%. (Those describing themselves as "neither" did not increase at all, holding steady at 6%).

For Christianity, the world's largest religion, this sounds like bad news. But perhaps it's not. As Dr. Bruce Shelley, the church historian, says, Christianity has always been a religion of the Spirit.[42] "Life in the Spirit" is a major

---

42 *Church History in Plain Language*, 2nd edition (Thomas Nelson, 1995), p 64.

theme in Paul's explanation of essential Christianity, so this one is right in our wheelhouse. To be a Christian—a genuine Christian—is a profoundly spiritual experience. So if you've walked away from Christianity because you think of yourself as a spiritual person and therefore you are looking for something beyond the sterile ritualism or moral bloviating you experienced at a church, I have good news: Paul describes essential Christianity as union with God—not just in the sense of a legal reconciliation with him, but a *relational* reunion with him by his Spirit.

In fact, in Romans 8 Paul makes fellowship with that Spirit the test of whether you are truly a Christian (Romans 8:9). "Life in the Spirit" is his shorthand for the Christian life. He tells the fledgling Roman church that fellowship with the Spirit is the gateway to "life and peace" (Romans 8:6), and tells his younger protégé, Timothy, that the Spirit is how he can thrive in power and love and self-control (2 Timothy 1:7). Jesus went so far as to tell his disciples that having the Holy Spirit inside them would be better than if he remained beside them (John 16:7). In other words, our experience with the Spirit is supposed to be so incredible that if we could choose between having Jesus physically in front of us or the Spirit inside us, we'd choose the Spirit![43]

If Paul's first theme in Romans is that we can only be made right with God through the finished work of Christ, his second is that we can only live out our new relationship with God by the power of his Spirit.

---

43 This is the core premise of my book *Jesus, Continued* (Zondervan, 2014).

WHAT DOES THE SPIRIT DO?

Maybe you think of communing with the Spirit as hearing whispered messages or getting overtaken by waves of warm fuzzies. There are certainly places in the Bible where the Spirit manifests himself in demonstrative ways, but Paul's focus in Romans is on how the Spirit assists us in our growth toward Christ-likeness. Here are a few things Paul identifies.

The Spirit Enables Us to Believe in Jesus

Paul says, "Anyone who does not have the Spirit of Christ does not belong to him. But if Christ is in you ... the Spirit is life" (Romans 8:9-10). If someone truly trusts in Jesus, the Spirit has to be present. Paul told the Corinthians, in fact, "No one can say 'Jesus is Lord' except in the Holy Spirit" (1 Corinthians 12:3). Without transformation by the Spirit, our hearts resist and suppress the truth that Jesus is Lord. The Spirit has to open the eyes of our hearts so that we see Jesus for who he is and feel our deep need of him.

Think of it like this: imagine a man who's lost his marbles standing on the top of a skyscraper, convinced he is Spiderman. He is about to jump, cast his web, and swing to the next building. I come up behind him and say, "Don't do that. You are not Spiderman." Because he is unable to tell reality from fiction, he will likely spurn my warning and jump. Now imagine I had a magic wand with which I could restore to his sanity to him. I could issue the exact same warning, using the same words, and this time he'll back away from the ledge. Nothing changed in my invitation; what changed was the condition of the mind that heard it. In a similar way, the Spirit of God restores our spiritual sanity so that when we hear the truth about Jesus, it becomes not just believable but irresistible.

The Spirit Produces the Life of Christ in Us

Paul says repeatedly throughout Romans 8 that the Spirit in us is *life*. In his letter to the Galatians, Paul lists out "spiritual fruit" (evidences of spiritual life) that the Spirit produces in the lives of those whom he indwells: things like love, joy, peace, patience, kindness, goodness, faithfulness, gentleness, and self-control (Galatians 5:22-23). These things only grow in us through the Spirit.

Trying to work these things up *without* the Spirit is like trying to get a dead rosebush to produce living roses. Some years ago, my wife asked me to beautify the flowerbeds in our front yard—specifically by killing the weeds. I soaked the ground around the rose bushes in herbicides, and in the process killed all the rose bushes. Wife not happy.

Now imagine I had told her, "Nothing to fear, Roni" and had run out to the florist, bought a few dozen roses, and stapled the fresh buds onto the dead limbs. Then every couple of weeks I'd repeated the process. From a distance, the rosebushes would have looked alive and healthy, covered with beautiful, colorful rosebuds. But it would've just been an illusion, and a tiring one to maintain.

Trying to live the Christian life apart from the Spirit is as exhausting as continually stapling fresh rosebuds onto a dead rosebush. When the Spirit of God is at work in you, however, he produces this spiritual fruit as naturally as beautiful flowers grow on a living rosebush. As long as the bush has deep roots in healthy soil and stays showered with sun and rain, flowers grow naturally. In the same way, the more you commune with the Spirit, the more fruit he produces in you.

The Spirit "Sheds Abroad" Christ's Love in Our Hearts

This is a phrase that Paul uses in Romans 5:5 and expounds in chapter 8. "Sheds abroad" means more than "to convince you propositionally about the facts of God's love." Paul is pointing to a *felt experience* of being overwhelmed by God's love. In doing this the Spirit *bears witness* with our spirit that we are the children of God.

Paul says, "You have received the spirit of adoption as sons, by whom we cry, 'Abba, Father'" (Romans 8:15-16). He is referring to a sense of intimacy we feel with the Father, welling up deep from within. Virtually every language in the world has two words for father. There's the more formal one—"father." Then there's a far less formal one: one that implies tenderness and closeness—like "Daddy" (English), *Papa* (Spanish), *Bapa* (Indonesian), *Baba* (Turkish), and so on. *Abba* is that word in Aramaic. The Spirit of God makes God feel like a tender Father.

My dad loves to tell a story about the first night he took me overnight camping. Apparently I slept all night with my hand on his belly. The next morning he asked me why I'd done that, and I answered, "I was afraid that I might wake up in the middle of the night alone out here in the woods, with the bears."

Deep down, I think we still live with that kind of fear, even as adults—the fear of being on our own, without someone to love and care for us, exposed to the "bears" that life throws at us. But just as my dad would never have left me in the woods, every Christian has a heavenly Father who will never leave them. The Spirit makes us aware of that truth, reminds us of it, and helps us feel it.

Maybe you find it difficult to get your mind around the presence of a never-leaving heavenly Father because your earthly dad did exactly that—he left you, ignored you, or abused you. It can be very tough for people to warm to the idea of God as Father if their earthly fathers let them down. But when we look at how God treats his people, we learn what fathers are supposed to be like. In God we experience a welcoming, kind, gentle, protecting, loving Dad. Instead of seeing our heavenly Father through the lens of our earthly one, we should try to evaluate our earthly dads through the lens of our heavenly one.

The Spirit wants to produce in you these *feelings* of intimacy with the Father. Truly, this is the essence of what it means to be filled with the Spirit! D. Martyn Lloyd-Jones, the renowned 20th-century Welsh pastor of Westminster Chapel in London, had a great illustration for this. (I've adapted it to my own life.) Imagine I'm walking along the sidewalk with my 5-year-old daughter, Ryah. I look down at her and think about how cute she is and how much I love her. So I pick her up and spin her around and blow raspberries in her neck. She blushes and says, "Oh, Daddy, you're so silly."

Was Ryah any more my daughter in *that* moment than she was the moment before? Legally, no. Was I any less committed to her? No.

But at that moment, when I picked her up, she *felt* my presence in a special way. She *knew*, in an intimate and experiential way, that she is my child. *This* is what the

Spirit does when he "bears witness with our spirit that we are children of God." He sheds abroad—some translations say "pours out"—God's love in the believer's heart, so that we overflow with it. These feelings don't happen every time we pray, but the still, small voice of the Spirit is there, quietly directing us to God's promises in times of need and assuring us of our place in his heart.

The Spirit Prays for Us

Paul points out one more important thing the Spirit does in our day-to-day lives. He says, "We do not know what to pray for as we ought, but the Spirit himself intercedes for us with groanings too deep for words" (v 26). There are times when a Christian feels so weak, so confused, and so overwhelmed that we don't even know what to say. In those moments, the Spirit speaks for us. "Groanings too deep for words" is a mysterious phrase, and we probably don't know the half of what it means. But two things are for sure.

First, the Spirit feels our emotions. "Groaning" is an emotional term. In John 11, Jesus showed up at the tomb of Lazarus, a recently deceased friend. He was there to raise him back to life, but first he stood at his friend's tomb with Martha and Mary, Lazarus' grieving sisters, and in the shortest verse in the Bible, we read this: "Jesus wept" (v 35). Didn't Jesus know that within an hour, he'd have raised Lazarus back to life? Yes, but still he wept. Why? Because his friends were weeping, and that's what you do when someone you love has their heart broken. You weep with them.

The Spirit of God does in a Christian now what the Son of God did with his friends then. He groans with you in your time of pain. Sometimes, during deep suffering, I find great comfort in knowing the Spirit is right there with me, feeling my pain. Sharing it. Bearing it. Groaning with me.

Second, "groaning too deep for words" means he's praying with wisdom that is impossible for me to grasp or express in human nouns and verbs. There are times when we don't know what to pray—when all we can say to God is "I don't know why this is happening, I don't know what you're trying to do here, and I don't even know what to say to you right now." At that moment, the Spirit of God prays for us. He takes our groans and translates them into specific requests for God to accomplish good in and through our life.

My first pastor was one of the godliest men I've ever known, and a great man of prayer. When someone asked him for prayer, he would say, "Of course, I will pray for you—but more importantly, the Spirit will, too. And when I say 'Amen,' he continues."

THE FUTURE IS COMING

One day, for those who trust in him, Jesus will bring the same renewal to our bodies that the Spirit has brought to our souls. The Spirit's presence in our hearts now assures us that redemption is coming for our bodies. In the meantime, the Spirit reminds Christians that we are "fellow heirs" with Christ. All that Jesus has coming to him, we have coming to us.

Let's stop for a moment and think about all which that includes. First, Paul says, *a perfected world*. "Creation itself will be set free from its bondage to corruption and obtain the freedom of the glory of the children of

God" (Romans 8:21). Sin did not just spoil humanity; it spoiled our world. But one day the resurrected Jesus will heal our world in the same way he is healing our spirits. What's the "healed" Hawaii going to look like? What does a curse-free donut taste like? I don't fully know yet, but I can't wait to find out.

Second, *a perfected body*. Paul says we Christians "wait eagerly for ... the redemption of our bodies" (v 23). Right now, we have bodies that ache, get sick, and break. It seems that every day I discover some new part of my body that can hurt. In the morning, I wake up sore, and all I did the night before was sleep! Somehow, rolling from my back to my right side has messed me up for the day. One day, Paul says, Jesus will set us free from this broken body and give us new ones—heavenly bodies, like his, that enjoy meals, don't get sick, don't hurt, walk through walls, and fly (see John 20:26; Acts 1:11)! I can't prove this, but I'm pretty sure we will be able to eat all the bacon and ice cream we want, while kale and alfalfa sprouts will make us gain weight.

Perfect bodies in a perfect world—I can't fully imagine either of those things, but I'm ready for them. Whatever the future is, Paul tells me that "what no eye has seen, no ear has heard, and no human heart has conceived— God has prepared these things for those who love him" (1 Corinthians 2:9, CSB). That means if you can imagine it, it's not good enough. And the best thing, of course, is that we're in the presence of Jesus and a throng of people who love him.

The Spirit in us assures Christians of this future, reminding us that it's worth any cost, any pain, and any sacrifice to stay faithful to Jesus. "I consider that the sufferings of this present time are not worth comparing with the glory that is to be revealed to us," Paul tells the Romans (Romans 8:18). Whatever pain I go through here is not even worthy of being compared to the joy that awaits me there.

Paul says to the Christian, *Hang on. We're almost there.* Lean into the Spirit. He'll carry you home.

LIVING IN THE SPIRIT

God did not leave us on our own to try and figure out this Christian life thing on our own. He gave us the Spirit. If we fail to lean into him, we'll never make it. Paul says,

> "If you live according to the flesh [that is, by the power of the flesh] you will die. But if by the Spirit you put to death the deeds of the body, you will live."
> (Romans 8:13)

We can only defeat the power of sin by the superior force of the Spirit. Trying to fight sin in the power of your flesh is like open-hand-slapping a bear—it doesn't matter how well you start, it isn't going to end pretty. To overcome the power of death in you takes the power of resurrection life.

Maybe you ask, "What does it mean, practically speaking, to live by the power of the Spirit?" How do we access that power? Do you close your eyes and channel your energy, like Luke Skywalker summoned the Force in Star Wars? Do you quote Bible verses, recite prayers, and hum worship songs?

Living in the Spirit simply means walking with the Spirit, and here are four things the New Testament tells us must be part of our lives if we are to do that.

Confession: God can heal any sin, but we must first expose it. Sin is like mildew: it grows in darkness, but bring it into the sun and it goes away. We trigger the power of the Spirit by confessing our sin—first to God and then to each other.

Surrender: The Spirit is not a force to master that we can deploy like a weapon. The Spirit is a person we must surrender to. When we say no to him, even about small things, we cut ourselves off from his power. Disobedience is like unplugging an appliance from an electric outlet. The moment the connection is severed, the power is gone.

Saturation: This is an important one. The Spirit breaks sin's hold on us by reminding us of our full acceptance with the Father. Re-believing the gospel releases in us the power of the Spirit. That's why Paul started his section in Romans on the Spirit by reminding us that "there is ... no condemnation for those who are in Christ Jesus" (8:1). As we dwell on the "no condemnation" that God has given us in Christ, the Spirit's power surges in us. The deeper we go in the gospel, the stronger we grow in the Spirit.

Memorization: This enables us to call to mind gospel promises when we need them. When Jesus fought the devil, he confronted particular temptations with specific phrases from the Scriptures (Matthew 4:1-11). It's how he stayed "in the Spirit." Paul calls Scripture the "sword of the Spirit" (Ephesians 6:17), and quoting it is how we leverage the power of the Spirit against our enemy. Trying to do battle with sin without a thorough knowledge of Scripture is like going into a gunfight without bullets.

Those four things—confession, surrender, saturation, and memorization—are how a Christian keeps in step with the Spirit and experiences his power.

NO BRAKE PEDAL

If the Spirit were merely a force, perhaps we could master a few techniques to harness his power. But he's not. He's a person, who comes to take up residence in our hearts as Lord. To experience his power, you have to fellowship with him, and you can only fellowship with him from the posture of total surrender.

When I was learning to drive, my driving instructor's car had a brake pedal in the front-passenger side, so that he could stop the car anytime he wanted. I remember I was about to roll through a stop sign when he slammed on the brake. In that moment he showed me that my sense of control over that car was an illusion. He could stop the car anytime he wanted to.

Many of us want to walk with God like that. We are happy for the Spirit of God to be an influence in our lives—to be a guide, an encourager, a help in times of trouble—but we want to retain access to that brake pedal.

To surrender means to cut that brake cable—to say to the Spirit, "Wherever you want, whenever you want, however you want—you lead, I'll follow."

Cutting the brake cable is scary. But, as Paul says, it's the only way to "life and peace" (Romans 8:6), and how you experience the most abundant life available to mankind—the gospel-centered life, the life you were created for.

That's what it means to be led by the Spirit—and it's how you become truly spiritual.

THEREFORE

Now What?

"I appeal to you therefore, brothers, by the mercies of God…" (Romans 12:1)

Some words change your life forever:

"You've been accepted."

"Marry me."

"I'm pregnant."

These are words that don't merely inform us—they transform us.

Paul's "therefore" at the beginning of chapter 12 is one of those words.

The book of Romans divides into two major sections. Romans 1 through 11, which we've been exploring, lays out what the gospel *is*.[44] Starting in chapter 12, Paul then begins to explain how the gospel enables us to live.

---

44 Of course, we've had to leave a few parts out. If you want to study them in greater depth, check out Tim Keller's *Romans 1 – 8 For You* and *Romans 8 – 16 For You* (The Good Book Company, 2014/2015); or my RightNow Media video series ("The Book of Romans," https://app.rightnowmedia.org/en/content/details/750879).

He joins these two sections by a single word—a word that marks not only the hinge point of Romans, but unlocks the secret of the Christian life itself:

> "**Therefore**, *brothers and sisters, in view of the mercies of God, I urge you to present your bodies as a living sacrifice, holy and pleasing to God; this is your true worship. Do not be conformed to this age, but be transformed by the renewing of your mind.*"
> (Romans 12:1, my emphasis, CSB)

Christian living is a response to what we've found in the gospel. *Therefore*—in light of who Jesus is and what he's done—we should think and live differently. Paul loads this verse up with a number of important words—words that encapsulate essential Christianity. Let's carefully pull out each of these sticks of dynamite, one at a time.

"WORSHIP"

Sin, as we've seen, starts as a worship problem. We give non-God things God-like weight in our hearts.

Eric Geiger, reflecting on the work of the Christian counselor David Powlison, groups our primary idols into four basic categories, calling them "root" idols:

Approval: We want to be accepted by others, so we become a slave to the opinions of others. We live by their praise and die by their criticism. We make ourselves into whatever others want us to be, to earn their love and respect.

Power: We love the feeling of superiority, so we pursue those things we believe give it to us, be that money, good looks, status, popularity, or positions of influence. We're willing to do whatever it takes to get them. We become prone to ruthlessness, dishonesty, and a tendency to treat people like pawns.

Control: In order to feel safe, we need things to go according to our plan. So we attempt to dominate the people and circumstances around us. We worry constantly. If others don't do what we want them to do, we become irritable and angry. If things don't happen according to our timetable, we become impatient, angry, even abusive.

Pleasure: We worship sensual pleasures—sexual pleasures, creature comforts, good food, a life of leisure, or alcohol or drugs, for example—so we organize our lives around pursuit of them. If we have to break God's laws to get them, so be it. We fear boredom. Worshiping pleasure often leads to irresponsibility, laziness, and compulsive behavior.[45]

Until God uproots those idols—until he becomes the one whose approval we seek, whose power we trust in, whose control we depend on, and whose pleasure we live for, any changes we make to our behavior are superficial and short-lived. Think of it as like trying to bend a four-foot metal beam. Pushing as hard as you can on either end, you might bend it a little, but it would stay bent only while you maintained the pressure. It would get tiring. Put too much pressure on the beam and it will break.

Trying to conform our sinful hearts to God's commands yields the same results. The hard, brittle metal of our hearts just won't bend toward God's laws, so we

---

45 "Four Root Idols," October 1, 2013; https://ericgeiger.com/2013/10/four-root-idols/ (accessed July 7, 2022).

inwardly seethe, resenting God for being such a ruthless taskmaster, or we give up, concluding that we are just not cut out for the Christian life.

Take a blowtorch to that beam, however, and you can bend it into whatever shape you want. The gospel is the blowtorch that melts our hearts so that they can be "conformed" to the image of Christ. As we've seen throughout this book, God is not just after obedience, he's after a whole *new kind* of obedience: an obedience that grows out of desire—an obedience in which we seek God because we crave God and pursue righteousness because we delight in it.

Until we change what we crave—what we *worship*—we'll never be able to truly stop sinning. We may conform our behavior for a while, but our hearts will pull the other direction. As Paul Tripp says, "If we worshiped our way into sin, we have to worship our way out."

The only power that can change what we worship, at the heart level, is the gospel. That's why Paul says that the gospel, and the gospel alone, is "the power of God for salvation" (Romans 1:16). The gospel does what no law, no matter how perfect or winsomely presented, can do—it changes us.

"TRANSFORMED"

This brings us to the word "transformed." The word Paul uses in Romans 12:2 is *metamorphoo*, and it's where we get "metamorphosis," the word we use to describe what happens to a caterpillar after it wraps itself up into a cocoon. I'm not an expert on butterflies (though I have read *The Very Hungry Caterpillar* many, many times), but as I understand it, when the caterpillar is in the cocoon, it isn't in there reading flight manuals and working on its wing muscles. The caterpillar's body releases enzymes that turn its little body into a gooey soup, and then its cells rearrange themselves into a new form—a form now with wings, antennae, and all the rest. This new creation then nibbles a hole in the cocoon and, without any classes, coaching, or coercion, soars away in flight.

I'm not sure how much Paul knew about butterflies, but something similar happens when someone becomes a Christian. At conversion, God releases "gospel enzymes" into your heart, which restructure it so that spiritual flight becomes second nature. You no longer grub along in tortured obedience to the demands of religion; you soar in Christlikeness because you feel like that's what you were created to do. You've been transformed.

This is *fundamentally* different from religious change. Religion tries to change us *mechanically*—coercing us to conform our behavior to the demands of that religion. But imagine the caterpillar tried to change that way: in the cocoon it reads a book on flying and then straps on some wings. Imagine how short and miserable its aerial adventure would be. Its untransformed caterpillar body just wasn't designed for flight.

Maybe that describes you spiritually: always trying to coerce yourself to do something you feel incapable of doing. You're exhausted.

In the gospel, God offers a different kind of change— not a correction of behavior but a transformation of the heart.

"REASONABLE"

The next key word is "reasonable." When the gospel has produced that transformation in us, offering our bodies to God as a living sacrifice starts to seem like the reasonable thing to do. ("Reasonable" is a translation of the word Paul uses that our Bibles translate as "true" or "spiritual" worship: *logiken*. It's where we get our word "logical.") In other words, full surrender just makes sense.

Surrendering your life to Jesus is not easy. It means dying to controlling your own life. *If* you know you've received grace from God in the gospel, however, even that feels reasonable. After all, God loved us enough to become a man and lay down his life for us. When we spurned him, he sought us. When we forsook him, he forgave us. He's the God who not only created us but redeemed us when no one else would have—why wouldn't we want to offer our lives to him?

C.T. Studd was one of English cricket's greatest players. In the late 1800s, cricket was a huge worldwide deal, so Studd was his era's LeBron James. And then one day, at the height of his career, he just quit: not to sit on a beach in France but to serve as a missionary in China. People asked him why. Why walk away from so much for so seemingly little? His answer came right from Paul's "therefore" in Romans 12:1:

> "If Jesus Christ be God and died for me, then no sacrifice can be too great for me to ever make for him."

"LIVING SACRIFICE"

Paul says that following Jesus means offering your life as a "living" sacrifice. The problem with a "living" sacrifice, of course, is that the sacrifice always wants to get up off the altar! To be a "living sacrifice" means a daily re-surrendering of our lives.

When I was 16, I went to a youth camp where, on the last night, we were invited to grab a stick representing our lives, walk up, and throw it on the bonfire. It was supposed to represent our decision to die to our control of our own lives. I remember how difficult it was to step out, take that stick, and throw it into the flames. But that was the easy part. The difficult part has been renewing that surrender day in and day out.

To be frank, many who decide to "get religious" aren't looking for this daily death to self. They want God to be an accessory in their lives, but they are not looking for total surrender to him. And yet, Jesus is clear: following him means a total surrender—being ready to do whatever he wants you to do, say whatever he wants you to say, and go wherever he wants you to go.

Years ago there was a popular bumper sticker which read, "God is my co-pilot." Here's the reality: if God is your co-pilot, then somebody's in the wrong seat. To follow Jesus means that you acknowledge that the car belongs to Jesus and surrendering the keys to him. You then hop in the back seat and say, "Ok, Jesus, where are we going?" Jesus comes only as Lord, never as cosmic assistant.

And what is our motivation to do that? Because, as Paul says, after we understand the gospel, it just *makes sense*. Who else would we trust with our lives? If the gospel is true, what else is worth living for?

And then, after we surrender to Jesus, we join the countless numbers of people who have found that Jesus is what they've been searching for all along. Jesus, because he's our Creator, is the only one who can satisfy the cravings of our hearts. He's better than all the idols we tried to replace him with.

Jesus is more secure than money. God promises to supply all our needs according to his riches in Christ Jesus, and his stock never crashes.

Jesus is more fulfilling than romantic love. The arms we searched for in romance (that is, those feelings of tenderness and security) were actually his arms. He was who our hearts craved.

Jesus is stronger than earthly power. What greater power can there be than a sovereign God who has promised to commandeer every molecule in the universe for your good?

Jesus is more enduring than earthly achievement. Hearing "Well done, good and faithful servant" upon entering eternity (Matthew 25:21) is far more gratifying than receiving 100,000 trophies on earth, which begin to fade from people's memories as soon as they are awarded.

Jesus is more precious than physical wellness—he offers abundant life no matter the circumstances, and promises eternal life that can never be taken away.

Every other god we pursue disappoints. I know the experience of finally achieving something I've pursued for years, only to have it fail to live up to my expectations. You probably do, too. For a while the new romance filled you with excitement. The new job made you feel important. The pay raise gave you a real sense of security. But then those feelings wore off and left you, again, feeling...

Empty.

Vulnerable.

Exposed.

You feel like the Fortune 500 CEO who said, "I spent my whole life climbing the ladder of success, only to get to the top and find out it was leaning against the wrong building."

Paul asked the Romans, *You see where sin and worshiping something that isn't God led you, don't you? Why do you keep going back there? The wages, the payment, the result of sin is death—both living and eternal. Only the gift of God in Jesus yields eternal life, experienced both now and in the age to come* (Romans 6:21-23, my paraphrase).

A friend of mine moved to a new city where dog racing was popular. He told me that the best moment of every race was right before the start, when the announcer called out, "Heeeere's Rusty!" and a fake rabbit popped up on the track and shot along a little railway down the straightaway. "Man, when those dogs saw Rusty, they lost their mind," he said. "They'd start banging up against the doors of the cages, barking and jumping, and when they let down those gates, those dogs tore off after that fake rabbit like they'd been fired out of a cannon." They'd chase that fake rabbit all the way to the end of the track, he said, when suddenly "Rusty" disappeared back into a hole in the ground.

My friend said, "I'm sure, later in the kennel, the dogs were like 'Ahhh, I was so *close* this time!' And their dog friends are like, 'Gosh, *me* too! You think we'll ever see that rabbit again?'" And sure enough, the next day, *Rusty's back*! And so they chase him again, only to have him disappear again. And they repeat this again and again every weekend.

"Before we say, 'What dumb dogs!'" my friend added, "consider this: everyday our alarm clock goes off, and it's almost like that clock is saying, 'Heeeere's Rusty!' And out we go in pursuit of him."

The thing that's the saddest, my friend told me, is not the times when the rabbit disappears, but those moments when one of the dogs actually catches Rusty. He chews through it and... "Hey... wait a minute," he realizes. "I've been duped. This isn't even a real rabbit." My friend told me that if that ever happens, that dog never runs in quite the same way again.

Some of us have caught our version of Rusty. We moved into the house, obtained the corner office, or bought the car. But still we're... empty. What's next? We look for another Rusty. "Well, this Rusty is not what I thought it would be," we figure, "but I'm sure *the next one will be!*"

Jesus is the only God who can satisfy you. And the amazing thing is, you don't even have to chase him. He came after you.

Tim Keller says that perhaps the most amazing thing about God is that he is not only the God who, if you find him, satisfies you; he is also the God who, when you fail him, forgives you.

The idol of money says, "Fail to obtain me and you'll be miserable." The idol of control says, "Lose me and nothing in your life will work out for you." The idol of approval says, "Fall out of favor with me and you'll have no significance at all."

Jesus says, *You did fail me, lose me, and fall out of favor with me. But I still came and died for you. I'm here for you. You deserve wrath; I offer you eternal joy.*

All of us offer our lives to something. When we see what kind of God Jesus is, who or what else would we want to offer our lives to? Giving ourselves up to Jesus is *logical*. It's *reasonable*.

It's worship.

RENEW, RENEW, RENEW

All this brings us back to the word "therefore." The change God is looking for—the transformation of what we worship—happens through the power of the gospel. That power comes into us not because we believed the gospel one time, but because we continue to believe it day by day. As we *renew* our minds in the gospel, again and again, the power of new life becomes a reality.

As we've said throughout this book, the gospel is not just the diving board off of which we jump into the pool of Christianity; it's the pool itself. The deeper you go into the gospel well, the sweeter and purer the water becomes.

Martin Luther was right: to progress in the Christian life is always to begin again. The gospel is not just for unbelievers; it's for Christians, too.

So, Paul says, *Renew, renew, renew!* When you feel that you lack the motivation to keep offering yourself to Jesus, renew yourself in the "mercies of God" (12:1). When you lack the power to resist temptation, renew, renew, renew! Soak yourself in gospel truths until they ooze out of every pore of your being. When your soul is hungry, feast on the gospel. When the world suffocates you, breathe in the gospel. When life cuts you, bind yourself up with the gospel.

The deeper you go in Christ, the higher your heart soars. The more you are soaked in the fuel of the gospel, the brighter you'll burn for Jesus.

LOOK AT HIM

As we close this book, I want to ask you to do something, whether you've been a Christian for years or you're still considering this Christianity thing:

Look at Jesus, and think about who he is and what he did.

- In 1,000 years, will anything matter more than what he thinks of you? In 10,000?

- Has there ever been anyone who loved you like he does?

- Could there be anyone else who offers you as much, now and eternally?

The gospel is this:

God, in an act of grace, sent his Son, Jesus, to earth as a man so that through his life, death, and resurrection he could rescue us, reign as King, and lead us into the eternal, full life we were created to enjoy.

That is an announcement that you cannot treat casually. It's either the world's greatest offer or the world's cruelest hoax.

If the gospel is true, the only reasonable response is to say, with joy and abandon, whether for the first time or the thousandth time, "Jesus, you alone deserve my worship. I am yours."

Are you ready to say that?

AFTERWORD

I can remember the first big decision I ever had to make—I was nine years old and in the third grade at Sandhills Elementary school. The teacher was telling me that two amoeba happened to hit in a muddy puddle of water two million years ago and I was the result. That didn't sound good to me—she was saying that I was an accident.

Thank goodness I had a mother and grandmother who made sure I was in church every Sunday, and the pastor there told me something totally different—that there was an all-powerful, all-knowing, and all-loving God who reached down and knitted me together in my mother's womb. God had made me special and unique, and he wanted to have a personal relationship with me. I knew then that I was no accident, and I remember telling that pastor that I wanted a personal relationship with this God who had made me and loved me.

That's the first big decision I ever made, and it remains the most important one. And I have never regretted it, and never will.

In this book, my friend J.D. has taken the message that changed my life so many years ago, and he's shown how it can change yours, too. He's "put the cookies on the bottom shelf," so to speak. I've seen and experienced a lot in my years, on the football fields and in the NASCAR pit areas, but nothing comes close to the power of the gospel to redeem and transform. As you reach the end of this book, I'm confident you'll have found some answers to your deepest questions and that you'll have gotten your head around the simple message at the heart of Christianity.

Maybe you've been a Christian for a good while already— be sure to let the gospel reignite your passion for God and your joy in all he's given you.

Maybe you're a seeker—to you I'd like to ask the question I ask lots of people: "What's life?" I've spent a large portion of my life on teams and building teams, on the football field and in the NASCAR pit areas, and so, unsurprisingly, I lean toward sporting metaphors. And I've come to the conclusion that life is like a game. I don't want to lose the most important game I'll ever play, and I don't want you to either.

What do we need to win at this game? I think we need a great Head Coach and we need a great game plan. I've stated that God made us and knows everything about us. He needs to be our Head Coach in this game called Life. Would an all-powerful God put us here to play this Game of Life without a game plan? I don't think so. He has given us the perfect game plan—his word— which gives us with everything we need to live a truly successful, satisfying life.

J.D., as he has tracked through Romans, has brought you face to face with the Head Coach's game plan and shown you what it would look like to be on his team—to put your faith in Jesus and become one of his people. Will you—to use the language of the sports in which I've spent my working life—make God your Head Coach?

Joe Gibbs,
Three-time Superbowl-winning Coach
of the Washington Redskins;
Owner of Joe Gibbs Racing NASCAR team;
Author of Game Plan for Life

ACKNOWLEDGMENTS

A book like this is not written during the course of a publishing contract, as primary influences began to assert themselves long before I had any inclination to write a book on Romans. My earliest memories are of my mother, a new believer at the time, instructing me in the ways of Jesus. She went home to be with the Lord during the writing of this book, and I can't wait to be reunited with her in heaven. I also think of my dad, who lived out the gospel in front of me my whole life and is the most consistently zealous evangelist I've ever known. I am confident that countless people in eternity will point to him as a primary influence in their being there, and I am one of them. I can still remember him telling me, early on in my ministry, to avoid all the foolish and secondary controversies and to "Just preach Jesus, son. Just preach Jesus."

I also owe a great debt to Steve Roberson, a faithful youth pastor, who called me back to the faith of my childhood when I was in high school; and Tim Keller, whose consistent gospel mentorship over the years—both from a distance and up close—led me to rediscover the beauty of the gospel; that the gospel is not just how we begin in Christ but how we grow in him. And that's not to mention the faithful saints of old whose influence can be felt on nearly every page of this book—Martin Luther, John Calvin, John Bunyan, C.S. Lewis and John Stott, just to name a few—and gospel friends like Clayton King, Chad Price, Trevin Wax, and Vance Pitman, who always remind me to stay focused on those things of first importance. "Only one life to live, 'twill soon be past; only what's done for Christ will last," as C.T. Studd so memorably put it.

I also have to mention the tireless efforts of the world's greatest and most patient editor, Carl Laferton. He did more than go the extra mile with me on this book—he ran a few extra marathons. It is clear that for him and his colleagues at The Good Book Company, this is not a job but a ministry and life passion, and one to which they consistently give their first and best. Thank you to Chris Pappalardo, whose servant-hearted and selfless efforts behind the scenes make everything I teach, write, or say so much stronger; Daniel Riggs, who chased down references long after the rest of us had gone to bed; Amy Whitefield and Curtis Andrusko, who just make everything better; and Aly, just for being awesome.

Huge thanks to my wife, Veronica, who often functions as something like a right tackle (in American football) in my life, keeping my schedule clear so that I can devote time to projects we believe God has called me to. She is my number one partner, confidante, advisor, editor, and ally in everything. And to our kids, Kharis, Allie, Ryah, and Adon: thanks for being patient with a dad you sometimes had to share with others. You remain my greatest earthly delight, and spending time with you remains my most enjoyable refuge.

rightnow MEDIA

FREE BIBLE STUDY VIDEOS

Because you have purchased this book, you also have free access to these exclusive Bible study videos—perfect for group study or personal devotions.

Scan QR code or visit:

rightnowmedia.org/promo/romans

FREE ACCESS

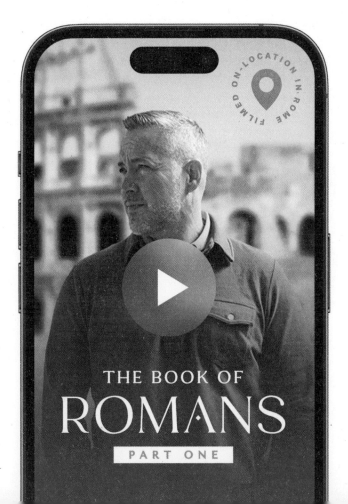

FILMED ON-LOCATION IN ROME

THE BOOK OF

ROMANS

PART ONE